MY HERO, MY SON

First Edition

ISBN: 1-4392-6728-6
Library of Congress Control Number: 2009912468

Joseph Baddick
Mohrsville, Pa.

To order additional copies, please contact
BookSurge/CreateSpace.

MY HERO, MY SON

JOSEPH BADDICK

2010

FOR LORRAINE,

ALL THE BEST - JOE

GOD BLESS

TABLE OF CONTENTS

This book is dedicated to my wonderful wife, Sheila, without whose love and gentle understanding, I might not have made it through my darkest hours.

ACKNOWLEDGEMENTS

I could never have written this book without the encouragement and assistance of Sharon Wells Wagner. It was with her guidance as an author that I was able to do something completely new to me. It was Sharon who helped conceive and nurture this project, and I thank her with all my heart.

I would like to thank Steve Wagner, Sharon's son, who assisted in polishing the manuscript, assisted with all the photos, and created the beautiful cover.

Thank you to my wonderful wife, Sheila, for all your help and for your company on the road trip to Louisville, Kentucky and Ft. Bragg to do interviews. For your encouragement that helped me continue on to the end, I thank you.

Many thanks to my daughter, Elizabeth, for the great stories you shared with me about your brother. I'm sure he would approve.

Thank you A.J. for being my son. Also, for all the hours we spent together trying to finish your book. I know that without your divine intervention, it never would have happened. Thank you for those times when suddenly out of the blue I was able to remember something about your past, when my mind was at a standstill. I knew it was your doing, because I asked.

Finally, to all our men and women in uniform, a special thanks for the sometimes thankless jobs you do. Where would our great country be without the sacrifices you make day in and day out? Thanks, also, to all those veterans who have served. God bless you and God bless America.

FOREWORD

There is a reason why I went into such detail about my time growing up, and the area of Pennsylvania where I grew up. It is also where my son, A.J. grew up. I wanted you, the reader, to get a feel for the type of environment and background that Sgt. Andrew Joseph Baddick came from. I can't imagine growing up in any other place, and I can only imagine that it positively influenced the type of man my son came to be.

INTRODUCTION

Early June nearly two years ago I was signing books at an event honoring World War II and its participants. This was my first book signing without my father, a WWII veteran and the subject of my book.

We had signed together, father and daughter inseparable, for nearly two wonderful years. Then in April, just five weeks earlier, he succumbed to lung cancer. My vibrant, brilliant, friend, and father was gone.

Needless to say, I was feeling sorry for myself, choking back tears as scores of people lined up to say they were saddened to hear of my loss. I'd handled his passing considerably well, even celebrated with close family members his "going home." But gazing into one sincere and loving face after another was more than I could bear. I wasn't going to make it through the day.

My self pity was abruptly interrupted when a dear friend, Ruth Gordon, tapped me on the shoulder from behind. She said, "Come here, I want to introduce you to someone."

Grateful for the interlude, I pushed back my chair, rose from my stupor, and followed her, stepping carefully around veteran heroes and chairs, books and WWII memorabilia, cluttered all together in a small but cozy aisle.

Ruth whispered. "I want you to meet my friend Joe Baddick. He's the one who lost his son in Iraq."

Lost his son in Iraq... My mind was suddenly reeling. The face of my own son, seated just a few feet away, flashed across my mind. Parents don't lose their sons. What was she talking about?

And then I saw him. Joe Baddick. A man with gentle, dark eyes and a smile I would never forget; a smile that was deep and loving, joyful and forgiving, a smile that was borne of healing. Instantly I knew. This man had lost his son, but not himself.

Ruth's joyful introduction of her dear friend, Joe, was completely lost on me. I didn't reach out for his hand, or respond in any polite manner. Instead, I embraced him. And in doing so experienced the greatest sense of loss I have ever felt in my life. My own sorrow now seemed inconsequential, petty, and even selfish compared to what this man had endured.

Joe and I quickly got acquainted as he spoke proudly of his son A.J. who'd been with the 82nd Airborne in Iraq. He spoke freely of the circumstances that lead to the young man's death. He had died trying to save the life of a fellow soldier.

"I remember reading about A.J. in the Reading paper," I told Joe. I was extraordinarily moved by the story. I felt a connection that I could not put my finger on. Ironically, Joe was more concerned with my recent loss, which by now I had completely forgotten.

By summer's end, Joe and his wife Sheila invited the Gordons and my family to their home for a picnic. In spite of the fact I'd known Joe for only a few weeks, I felt comfortable around him, was intrigued by his resilience, and looked forward to meeting the rest of his family. My connection to him was spiritual; I knew it without a doubt.

I also knew that our meeting was no coincidence. The crossing of paths is never without purpose.

And that picnic would prove me right.

Joe and I talked for hours about A.J. and dying, and life after death. We also discussed writing and publishing. We even visited Joe's self-described "man cave," a room dedicated to A.J., decorated with photos, citations and memories; a room where Joe could remember his son, or watch golf on TV and relax with a cigar, his little dog, Harry, by his side.

Returning to the subject of writing, Joe looked at me with a twinkle in his eye and said, "I want to write a book about World War II."

"No," I replied resolutely, as though I'd always known. "You must write a book about A.J." Not for Joe, I was certain, but for others who would lose their sons and daughters to war. And Joe agreed.

People fascinate me; their personalities, their quirks, their strengths, their joy, their sorrow, whatever makes them tick, and Joe was no exception. His resilience astounded me and his strength and courage inspired me.

How could one lose a child and continue to move courageously and productively forward?

"How did this happen?" I asked him hovering over Sheila's homemade blueberry pie. "How did you come to this acceptance, to this remarkably peaceful place in which you exist?"

Although Joe admitted that it was difficult at first, he looked me squarely in the eyes and spoke from his heart, "A.J. died doing what he loved; he was happy, and I'm okay with that."

I was almost convinced.

Then he continued, "And...I became a peer mentor. A.J was always helping others, and I know he would want me to do this."

The last piece of the puzzle fell into place. A peer mentor - an act of selfless giving.

Joe had not given in to his loss; he gave himself to others instead. He recalled stumbling across a copy of TAPS magazine and read an article about peer mentoring. With the encouragement of Sheila and his daughter, Elizabeth, Joe joined the Tragedy Assistance Program (TAPS), and volunteered to mentor other fathers who had lost their sons to war. He admits that each case reminds him of his own loss. And sometimes it gets very difficult, especially when a father harbors anger or guilt. But Joe does it anyway. He's taken heartbreak and transformed it into something good – helping other people. Exactly what A.J. did in his short lifetime. Like father, like son!

I never had the good fortune to meet A.J. Baddick, but I got to know him in the pages of this book, *My Hero, My Son*, the true story of a courageous and selfless young soldier.

Both father and son have taught me that courage is not the absence of fear or heartbreak, but the willingness to do whatever it takes to rise above it, particularly when helping another human being. That is the true essence of a hero.

God bless you A.J. Baddick!

Sharon Wells Wagner
Author of *Red Wells* & *Ordinary Heroes*

MY HERO, MY SON

THE COAL REGION

Chapter 1

This is the true story of Sgt. Andrew J. Baddick, an 82nd Airborne Division paratrooper, who made the ultimate sacrifice in Iraq.

It was October 1st, 2003. My wife Sheila and I were sleeping soundly when the telephone woke us at approximately one o'clock in the morning. I was about to receive the phone call every parent dreads. It was my daughter, Elizabeth, and from the sound of her voice I could tell something was wrong.

"Dad", she said, "A.J. is dead."

My voice trembling, I said, "what?"

"He's dead; A.J.'s dead." Even though I knew this was my daughter speaking to me, something in the back of my mind was telling me this could not possibly be true.

A voice I did not recognize now spoke to me. "Mr. Baddick, I am the chaplain assigned as liaison in this matter and it appears there was an accident involving your son Andrew and he drowned."

I told him, "that can't be; my son was an expert swimmer."
I told the chaplain there had to be a mistake...

Andrew Joseph Baddick was born on June 30th, 1977. We lived in Tamaqua, Pennsylvania at the time and I was working at the Atlas Powder Company, where we made dynamite and blasting caps. I was at work when a call came in advising me that I now had a son. After work I went to the hospital to see him. I was thrilled; what father wouldn't be? I was so happy and excited as I held this tiny little guy in my arms. I wondered what he would grow up to be. But I knew this, whatever he decided he wanted to be, he would have my support. My father never decided my future; he always supported me in my life choices. I would do the same for A.J.

My wife, Ann, and I already had a daughter and now having a son seemed to make everything come together. Life was good.

Later that night, I went out to celebrate with my friends, who, of course, bought me too many drinks in honor of my new son, A.J. I guess I celebrated a little too much because the next morning I went to work with a terrible hangover. I should have kept my ass in bed, but since we had to work the day before and the day after a holiday in order to get paid for the holiday, I went to work. I wanted to get paid for the Fourth of July.

You didn't go to your job at the Atlas Powder Company hung over, due to the nature of the work. I was working in one of the buildings when the foreman, Donny Krell, came in. As soon as he saw me, he told me to get out before I killed someone. He escorted me over to a building that wasn't running and told me to rake leaves into piles and bag them. I could have been fired for reporting to work in that condition but Donny Krell was my neighbor, a friend of my dad, Joe, and would become a second father to me.

I remember the day Ann and I took Elizabeth to visit my cousin, Rich Campbell, and his wife Verna. We were talking about children and the prospect of us having another one. I told them, "I don't think we are going to have another child."

Rich said, "Oh, that's too bad. You know, I'm an only child and all the time I was growing up I wished I had a brother or sister to play with."

I gave Rich's comment some thought and began to wonder what it would have been like without my older brother Guy in my life; lonely, I imagined. As time went on I became more receptive to the idea of having another child. Thank God I listened to my cousin.

Elizabeth was four years old now and had a new baby brother. Friends and relatives said that we now had a rich man's family, one girl and one boy. I was quite skeptical, and to this day I'm still waiting for the pot of gold at the end of the rainbow.

Andrew was named after my Grandfather. No one else in the family had named their son after him, so my aunts were very happy with the name we chose.

Elizabeth took to the job of big sister and seemed to enjoy it immensely. She would help out with baths, and she enjoyed brushing her brother's hair. A.J. had naturally curly hair and it was so soft. His mother let it grow nice and long to where he almost resembled a girl.

Elizabeth was quite a talker, and I wondered if little A.J. would take after her. I remember coming home from work one day and the minute I walked into the house, she started yelling, "daddy, daddy, daddy." I needed to get something down in the cellar, so I ran down the steps. Next thing I heard, at the top of the steps was Elizabeth calling down to me, "daddy, daddy, daddy."

I looked up the stairs and yelled, "Will you stop saying daddy?" My daughter's smile quickly faded, and she asked me, "Should I call you Joe?" That sure made my day and put a big smile on my face.

One warm afternoon Elizabeth went for a ride in the car with my parents, Rose and Joe, to Allentown, about forty miles away. On the trip home she was sitting in the rear of the car and her Gram turned around and said to her, "Elizabeth, come sit up front with us."

Her response was, "no, Pap's car is full of shit." My mother told me that five minutes later the car broke down. There were no cell phones in those days but fortunately they were close to a restaurant. My dad called me and I went and picked them up and brought them home. Where my sweet little daughter learned that phrase I'll never know. Seems she had a bit of ESP back then.

When Elizabeth was just a baby, I was in the Army and we were still living at Ft. Bragg, N.C. One night I was giving her a bath in a little tub that had a vinyl strip across it to lay the baby on. I had her lying on her belly and her mother came in the room and started screaming at me, "You're drowning her!" I was so intent on cleaning her legs I didn't notice her face was down in the water. Damn, bad daddy. I gave Elizabeth a kiss and told her I was sorry. We learn from our mistakes. However, she has me to thank for teaching her how to hold her breath under water.

When Elizabeth was very little she developed allergies. I remember one evening she was crying and crying, and her mother wanted to go in to her. I said that we should wait and that she would grow tired of crying and go to sleep. Well, it came to the point where I couldn't take it any longer and I got up and went in to her. There was my daughter sitting in her crib and she was a mess. She had thrown up all over the place. I felt like the world's biggest jerk. I picked her up and then went into the bathroom to fill the tub. I gave Elizabeth a bath and noticed she had broken out in a rash. I put clean clothes on her and then walked her until she fell asleep.

We took her to the doctor the next day and he suggested an allergist in Allentown. We made an appointment and took her for testing. We found out she was allergic to things in bloom, chocolate, dairy products, and certain beans. Well, it was spring and right outside her window lilac bushes were blooming. Then we had to find her milk that was non dairy and you could only buy it in Allentown at that time. Instead of chocolate, we would get her carob, a pretty good substitute. All things considered, she never complained about not being able to eat chocolate, and when we didn't have non-dairy milk, she would pour orange juice on her cereal and grew quite fond of it.

When school was in session I used to take turns with one of the neighbors dropping off our children and picking them up. I can recall a particular day when it was my turn to pick up the kids after school. I had been very busy and was out at the end of town buying something when I suddenly remembered that I had to get the kids. I looked at my watch and said, "holy shit!" I was ten minutes late. I drove the car at warp speed from one end of town to the other, and there, standing alongside of the school building, was Elizabeth and her little boy friend. The young lad was crying, and I watched my daughter put her arm around him and say, "See, I told you my dad would be here." I felt bad about that one - not for my daughter, but for her friend.

When Andrew was about four years old he had one of those riding toys called a Big Wheel. He would come tearing down the sidewalk on it and cut it into our alleyway. One day he was speeding toward our house when a neighbor, Mr. Kemery, stepped off his porch and A.J. knocked him right off his feet. I thought we were in for a lawsuit but all the neighbors loved A.J. Mr. Kemery got up and brushed himself off and told A.J. to be more careful in the future. I imagine Mrs. Kemery had to play nursemaid that evening.

We only lived a few blocks from the south ward playground and one particular day I took A.J. there. He was having a good time and asked if he could go down the big slide. I told him he could but to be very careful. The big slide was about twelve feet at the top. The area around the slide was blacktop, as was most of the playground. When A.J. got to the top of the ladder I told him to sit down. When he started down the slide he bent his knees and his sneakers caught the slide and stopped his downward momentum. He got scared and pushed himself forward, launching himself over and off of the slide. Even though I was standing at the bottom, I couldn't reach him fast enough. He did one complete flip and hit the blacktop. The back of his head hit with a terrible sound and I thought the worst. He was crying something fierce but I could see no blood. A few doors away lived a woman whose daughter babysat for us on occasion, so I went to see if she was home. She came to the door and I told her what happened, so she checked his head and said it appeared to be alright but I had better take him to the doctor to be safe. She asked A.J. if he wanted a Popsicle and he stopped crying and said "yes." The doctor examined A.J. and said he was fine. I suppose that was my son's first experience at being airborne. I chalked it up to our family genes; we are known to be hard heads.

Once when I was a young boy we were playing baseball and one of the guys decided to throw a rock at me, and it was a direct hit to the back of my head. I ran home crying, blood running down my back. My dad took me to the doctor who stitched me up and he told my dad I'd be okay.

One time our next door neighbor, Russell Kropp, was sitting on his front porch swing and A.J. came out of our alleyway with a bag over his shoulder. Mr. Kropp asked him where he was going. He said, "I'm running away from home." Mr. Kropp watched as A.J. went to the end of the block and sat down. A while later he returned and told Mr. Kropp he had changed his mind. Mr. Kropp invited A.J. up on the porch swing and treated him to a Popsicle. I don't remember what was bothering A.J. that particular day but I think Mr. Kropp and the Popsicle made it all better.

Joanne Myers was another one of our neighbors. Her house had the most unusual front steps. They were made of cement but not shaped quite right, so one had to be careful while traversing them. I believe her husband Charlie had a hand in their construction. Anyway, Joanne was coming down the steps and she tripped and fell. Andrew just happened to be near at the time and ran over to Joanne and helped her get up. Well, Joanne made a big deal out of it saying, "A.J., you saved my life." He felt so darn proud. From that day on it became a humorous topic between our families. We'd all be outside talking and the next thing you know, Joanne would say something like, "there's the kid that saved my life." A.J. would get a huge ear-to-ear grin on his face. I suppose A.J. was cut out for the business of saving lives. Unbeknownst to us all, it would become his destiny.

Back in those days it was common for me to come home from work, eat supper, then turn on the television and knock back a few beers. Of course, the time would come when nature called. As Archie Bunker once said, "you can't really buy beer, you can only rent it." I would put my half consumed bottle of beer on the end table and head upstairs to take care of business. By the time I returned I'd notice there was less beer in the bottle. I'd look at Elizabeth and A.J. and they'd start laughing. Now keep in mind, this wasn't a daily thing. When my aunt Genevieve heard about the kids drinking beer, she went ballistic and said, "You're going to kill the brain cells in their heads. You should be ashamed of yourself."

Elizabeth went on to graduate Magna Cum Laude with a nursing degree from East Stroudsburg University. I had a theory that the beer killed off the weaker brain cells to make room for new and improved ones, so I guess Aunt Gen wasn't entirely wrong. And A.J.? Well, he became a true fan of beer. It would become his very favorite beverage of choice, especially Yeungling Lager.

My dad would come get A.J. and take him to where they parked the railroad cars at the south end of Tamaqua. Andrew loved the trains. My dad would lift him up onto one of the cars and he would climb all over them. As a child, I loved trains too.

My parent's house, where I grew up, was located on Railroad Street. Back in the day it was referred to as Pleasant Row and it really was a pleasant street to grow up on. Out in front of the street were railroad tracks, so we all had a pretty good understanding of trains. I remember my mom telling us that during World War II, the troop trains would sometimes make a stop and all the neighbors would come out with sandwiches and drinks for the soldiers. The folks on our street would also wait for the trains to come by with open box cars or empty coal cars. They would toss their garbage into the cars. The box cars were more sporting because you had to lead them to get the bags in the open doors. As kids, we would put things like nails on the tracks and wait for the trains to run over them. They would be flat as a pancake. We also liked to walk the rails to see how far we could get before we fell off.

My father came home one day from the bar across the street called Tony Bells. They had punchboard games where you paid a nickel or dime and then punched out little pieces of paper with numbers on. My dad won a plastic slingshot and he gave it to me. My eyes lit up. Now keep in mind, to a little kid this was no ordinary slingshot, this was the deluxe model. It was red and stored ammo in the handle behind a small slide. My older brother, Guy, came over and said, "Let me see that." He jumped down on the railroad tracks and picked up a lead ball, about the size of a marble that they used in the coal cars. We lived next door to Eames Bakery, which was about three stories tall. Guy said, "Watch me launch this over the bakery." Well, it went right through a window with a tremendous crash that brought my father outside. Guy handed me the slingshot and took off. My dad asked where the noise came from and I just pointed at the broken window with slingshot in hand. That was the first and last time my beautiful red slingshot was ever fired. My dad took it out of my hands and stepped on it until it wasn't recognizable as a slingshot anymore. Oh well, easy come, easy go.

One day I took A.J. for a walk down to where my dad worked at a sheet metal fabrication plant called Remaly's so my dad could see him. My dad said it was soon time for his lunch break and for me to take A.J. over to the park about a block away. I had him on the swings when my dad started to head over toward us. It was cold out and my dad had to cross over an icy macadam basketball court to get to us. As I was watching my dad, his feet went out from under him and he came down, hitting the back of his head. I thought, "holy shit, he's dead." It's a damn good thing the Baddicks are hard headed. My dad lay there till I got to him and his eyes were open, so I asked, "Are you okay?" He said, "sure," rubbed the back of his head, and then got up and went over to A.J. and started pushing him on the swing as if nothing happened. My dad was one tough nut.

Growing up in the coal region was a real treat. Of all the places I've been, there is no place quite like it. Our house had steps going down to the basement and a wooden plank wall separated our house from the neighbor's. Our neighbors were Mary and Tony Lore and their daughter Dolly. I would go down the steps to the basement and there was a plank missing from the wall, so I would pass through and go up the Lore's steps. I would open the door, which led to their kitchen, and hear Mary say, "come on Joseph, sit at the table and I'll get you something to eat."

Tony would say, "Hello, wedge head." I don't know how he arrived at that particular name, but it stuck with me anytime I was around Tony.

Dolly was my babysitter. When my mom and dad would leave the house I would freak out, so Dolly had her work cut out for her. Once, I was so hysterical that I was hitting the back door right after my parents left and I cut my hand on the aluminum blinds that hung there. I was bleeding but Dolly took care of me.

I remember one of the things she did to soothe the savage beast in me was to have me lay across her lap as she lightly scratched my back. I loved it, and to this day I enjoy it when my wife Sheila does the same for me. I also remember that A.J. had a thing for having his back scratched and my mother would always accommodate him whenever he asked her.

My mom was a wonderful woman, and she had a humorous side to her. Once, when I was a little boy, she had this long screw driver in her hand and she told me to watch her. She did the old trick where you put your hand up to your mouth and pretend to slide the screw driver down your throat. I didn't seem to think it was funny though, I started yelling and crying, "take it out, take it out."

Another time she had a trick light bulb. She would put it in her mouth and it would light up. Now, that trick I thought was good; I liked it. To make it work you had to put a small piece of tin foil in your mouth and then touch the bottom of the bulb to it.

We had a Santa Claus face that lit up, and each Christmas my mom would hang it outside on the front porch. One time my dad said the wires were frayed and he had to re-wire it. My brother, Guy, was with my dad in the basement helping to fix the wiring. My dad told Guy to go upstairs and when dad yelled, Guy was supposed to plug it in.

Well, my mom was talking to Guy and my dad yelled something. Guy asked mom, "What did he say?"

My mother replied, "I think he said to plug it in."

Guy plugged the Santa Face into the receptacle and we heard a loud scream. It seemed my dad hadn't finished yet and was touching the bare wires. Mom thought it was funny. I think my dad lit up instead of the Santa face.

Another time, my dad and Guy were in the kitchen eating clams, and I went out to investigate what they were doing. I asked, "What are you doing?"

I did this a few times and each time my mother would say, "Don't you dare give Joseph one of those clams." Well, Guy looked at my dad with a devilish grin and they gave me a clam. I started gagging and then threw up. They caught hell from my mom for that one. Later on in life, however, I would develop a craving for clams and oysters.

Supposedly my mom was a pretty good tap dancer, and while I don't remember ever seeing her dance, she danced with me many times around the house and at weddings. She also belonged to the Catholic Women's Educational Association, or the C.W.E.A, at St. Jerome's Church.. They would regularly clean the church and host pinochle tournaments to benefit the school. They also set up the auditorium for first communion breakfasts and put on shows. They did a minstrel show in which my mom was Mister Interlocutor. If you ever saw the movie "White Christmas" they do a scene from a minstrel show which is similar.

There was this story about the time my mom and dad stood for Jimmy and Anna Mae Johnson when they got married. After the wedding, Jimmy and Anna Mae asked my mom and dad to join them on their wedding trip to New York City. While they were there, they went to eat at some really swank restaurant. My dad announced, "Order anything you like; tonight the meal is on me."

They ordered champagne and all the very best foods. When everyone finished the meal and the check arrived, my dad said he would take care of it. But first he had to use the restroom and would meet them outside in a few minutes.

A short time later, my dad showed up outside and said, "I think we should start running."

Jimmy asked, "Why?"

My dad replied, "Because here's the check!" My dad had ripped up the check and threw it into the air like confetti. Well, they ran and luckily they did not get caught.

Back in those days you could walk down Pleasant Row and go into just about anybody's house, unannounced, and be welcomed. No one locked their doors. We were all one big happy family. All the neighbors sat out on their front porches in the evening talking, while us boys and girls ran up and down the street playing kick the can or hide and go seek. We only stopped playing when we heard the ice cream truck coming down our street.

On hot summer evenings, my uncle Pete Campbell would sit out on his porch and play his trumpet. Man, he was good. He used to play with the Dorsey Brothers and Benny Goodman back in the day. When he played, all the neighbors came out to listen. Just imagine sitting out on a warm summer's night, with a cool drink, listening to "Stardust", which was his wife, Helen's, favorite, or "Moon River," and sometimes the Irish favorite, "Galway Bay." We were so fortunate to hear that kind of professional entertainment for free, and I will always remember my Uncle Pete because of it. He died when I was just a young boy. The world lost a great musician, and I lost an extremely talented uncle.

Tamaqua had its 125th anniversary in 1957 when I was only five years old. The whole town decided to celebrate with an Indian theme. The Indian translation for Tamaqua is "Land of Running Water." Each ward in the town represented a different Indian tribe. My family lived in the North Ward and we called ourselves the Hopi Indian tribe. Everyone dressed in Indian attire and the houses on our street were decorated with tepees. They were half tepees that you had to pass through to go into our houses.

There were railroad tracks between our street and the houses on the other side of the street. There was enough room next to the railroad tracks to erect an authentic Indian village. There were tepees, deer hides stretched on poles, a huge cooking pot suspended over a fire, and colorful blankets all around. Right across the street was Russ Ackerman's barber shop. He had it made up to look like the sheriff's office and he dressed just like a sheriff from the old west. I'll tell you, it was a big deal. You could travel all around the town and everyone was dressed like an Indian or cowboy. One day there was a huge parade and there were Indians and cowboys on horseback. My dad's boss was on horseback dressed as a cowboy. As he rode by, my dad remarked, "That's the first time I ever saw a horse's ass on top of the horse." That was Bill Yost. He was not only my dad's boss, but the town's mayor as well. Everyone cracked up at that one. It was one of the best times in town I can ever remember. You could never get a whole town together like that nowadays.

There was always good food to eat in our area because of all the different ethnic families. My dad and mom made their own kielbasa, stuffed peppers, pierogi, halushki, stuffed cabbage, bullet soup, city chicken, bleenies, hoagies, jellied pigs feet, and tripe. One of my dad's specialties was his hot baloney. His hot baloney became quite famous in the area. He made gallon jars for most of the bars to sell. He even told me that one time he was in a bar and some guy was eating his hot balonies and raving about them. He asked my dad if he could buy a couple jars to take back to Florida with him. My dad ran home and made the guy two jars, just like that.

There is another story about my dad's hot baloney. A.J. and I used to go to the Bowhunter's Festival at World's End State Park near Eagles Mere in Pennsylvania. This particular time we went with a friend named Mike Rascavage and his two young sons. We were to meet up with his brother, Dave, and another fellow. They went up early to set up the tent. Now, in a state park you may not have alcohol but when we arrived and went inside the tent, Mike's brother had set up a barrel of beer. I brought along a gallon jug of my dad's hot balonies. Dave had been drinking and loved hot baloney. He said, "watch this, I'll show you how a Marine eats hot balonies." With that he shoved the whole thing in his mouth and ate it, and then a few more. After we had all retired for the evening I was awakened by the sound of Mike's son's voice saying, "Dad, I have to pee." Mike told him to go outside by the tree to do his business. The young lad responded with, "I can't, there's a skunk out there." Well, we all got up by this time. It seemed that Dave, during the night, had gone out by the tree and threw up. The skunk was eating what Dave had regurgitated. Mike grabbed his son's arrows and was throwing them at the skunk to chase it away. I thought we would all get sprayed but that skunk refused to move until it ate all the puke. After what seemed like an eternity, the skunk took off, and there we all were, standing around that tree taking a leak. My dad's hot balonies were so good, even the animals enjoyed them.

The following year A.J. and I traveled to the Bow Hunter's Festival with Frank Umbriac, a good friend of mine from high school. Frank had a mobile home, an older model, and it didn't have a lot of "get up and go." The way to the Bow Hunter's Festival is all up hill, and very mountainous, so the going was quite slow. We dubbed the mobile home "The Tank." Man, it seemed like forever till we got there. I think Frank bought it from the "Slowskies." One thing I'll say in its favor is that it was a lot more comfortable than a tent. You see, A.J. and I had been there a few times before and it never failed to rain at least one day over the weekend, and we were always in a tent. The whole placed tended to get a bit muddy but we were usually prepared for it.

A.J. really enjoyed going because he loved to shoot his bow, and one of the targets was a running deer that would go back and forth on a rail, and the archers on the line, about forty of them, would all be shooting at this deer. When the horn sounded to stop shooting, the deer would be sent out to the center of the range. It was comical because there were dozens of arrows stuck in both sides of the deer. It resembled a giant porcupine. I have a video clip of A.J. standing on the firing line shooting at the deer.

There was a barn where they had people putting on exhibitions, and in the evening there was always a bluegrass band for entertainment. One time in particular that I remember, there was a guy there that was an expert with the crossbow. He had just put on an exhibition and was telling the audience just how easy it was to shoot a crossbow. To make his point, he asked a young boy to come out of the stands and join him. Now, there was a small room in one corner of the barn. The man with the crossbow was explaining how it worked and said he was going to have the boy shoot it momentarily. Just as he was saying, "now don't touch the........" the boy's finger found the trigger. The arrow shot out and luckily the man had it pointing away from the crowd. The arrow entered the small room and we heard it ricochet off the walls about three times. Needless to say, that was the first and last time that young boy fired the crossbow. It was just an all around good time for everyone there, especially for my son and me.

During hunting season we ate deer steaks, chops, and stews, as well as rabbit, squirrel, and pheasant. The barber across the street, Russ Ackerman, even made groundhog stew. And down at the end of our street was Mickey Padora's Italian Bakery. My mom would send me to get some Italian bread or rolls and I loved going there. I'd go inside and watch Mickey put the dough on these really long handled, wooden paddles, and then he would shove them way back inside the stone oven to bake. There was nothing state of the art in that bakery and it's still in operation today. Mickey would put the freshly baked warm bread in a bag and I'd head home, but the bread never made it without me breaking off a piece to eat along the way. Of course, I'd get yelled at, but it was worth it.

My brother, Guy, told me he and our cousin Rich Campbell, would stop by at Mickey's on their way to the movies. They'd buy a loaf of warm Italian bread, break it in half, pull a piece of the center out, and shove a stick of butter inside. By the time they got to the movies it was ready to eat.

I had other plans for Mickey's bread. I would always go to my grandmother Nora's house after school because both my parents worked. She was my dad's mother, and she had an old coal stove in the kitchen. I would cut a few pieces of bread, butter both sides, and place them on a screen she had for toasting. You had to remove one of the burners with a special handle and then put the screen over the hole. When one side was toasted, I would turn the screen over and toast the other side. When the bread was done toasting it would come off onto a plate and I would pour Turkey Syrup on it. That was a real treat back then.

A friend of my dad, George Dunstan, worked at the Atlas Powder Company. Each Tuesday George would take orders for hoagies and cheese steak sandwiches. On Tuesday evenings my mom and dad would be in the kitchen making up the orders, and of course, I had to lend a hand. Now, we're talking over a hundred sandwiches. I can still see my dad standing there cutting up all the onions he'd need. To prevent his eyes from tearing up he'd wear my swimming mask. He resembled The Creature from the Black Lagoon. My dad would sell the hoagies and cheese steaks at a marginal profit, but that's just another way my dad found to help out with household expenses. Mickey Padora's Italian Bakery is still pumping out bread and rolls to this day.

Friends of my dad would give him wild mushrooms in the fall. He would bring home a ram's head mushroom and my mom would chop it up and sauté it with onions in butter. That was some good eating.

My dad worked his regular job and after work he would tend bar part time at his friend's bar room to make ends meet. My dad was the kind of guy who loved to give stuff to people all the time. I could have had a yard sale and I'd have made a substantial profit from what he gave away, but that was just my dad's way; he had a good heart.

He had a chance to buy his friend's bar room, and I think he would have done a good business because he knew everyone in town and he and my mom made a lot of great homemade food that they could have sold. There were living quarters above the bar room too. However, my mom refused to live atop a bar room and she also said that my dad would have given food and drink away dirt cheap or for free. I tend to agree, he was a real giver.

Sometimes, when he would come home from being at a bar he would throw a whole box of Slim Jims at me, because he knew they were my favorite. After Sheila and I got married, my mom and dad came to visit and Sheila made the comment that she liked Peppermint Patties. Well, he got her a whole box of them, the little ones. Another time my dad knew our son-in-law, Rick, liked crab legs. Guess what, he bought Rick a whole box of them. My dad didn't have a lot of money to buy extravagant things, but what he bought was truly from the heart.

Another one of my dad's part time jobs was running numbers. You could say it was the lottery before it became legal in Pennsylvania. People would give my dad a three digit number to play and to put money on. I have one of my dad's old numbers books and listed in it are people's names and their number picks. There were times when the police would be on the prowl trying to catch my dad and others who did this because it was illegal.

My dad's sister, Kay, was a telephone operator and when she heard the police were on the lookout, she would warn my dad. Then my dad would give me or my brother a sandwich bag and tell us not to open it, but we were to deliver it to one of the neighbors. Inside it were betting slips. We would wait for the neighbors to put their numbers on the betting slips and deposit their money in the bag and then we would return home and give the bag to our dad.

One of my deliveries was to a woman by the name of Florence Linkevich, who lived a couple of streets away from us. Her sister Mary lived with her and she had a son named Joe, who was a few years older than I was. I always enjoyed going over there because Florence and Mary were so good to me. They would offer me anything in the house to eat or drink, and they were really nice people. Florence's husband, Joe, was a B-24 pilot who flew missions out of India. His plane crashed on September 5, 1945, a few days after VJ Day, Victory over Japan. Joe Jr. and I hadn't seen each other in many years, but for the last couple of years I have been golfing with a group of guys and wouldn't you know it, Joe is one of them. We've shared stories and Joe has even brought pictures of his dad from WWII for me to see.

Another tactic my dad employed was using my mom for deliveries. She would hide the betting slips in her bra, because my dad knew the police would never check there. Anyway, my dad had a few jobs in his day, some a bit questionable, but one thing I can say; my dad always made sure we had a roof over our heads, clothes to wear, and food to eat. He was a good provider no matter what lengths he had to go to.

My dad always dressed in a pocketed, button-down shirt so that he could put all his tickets and pens in the pockets. He usually had in one shirt pocket raffle tickets, a couple of pens, and his eyeglass case. I don't think you could have fit anything else in it. Sometimes it appeared as if my dad had a growth on his chest.

Some days, my dad would come home from work and, after a quick bath, he would tell my mom he was going out to the local bars to play the daily pool. The daily pool was ten cents and a person would write his name down. If you won, the next time you came in you got your money.

There were days when my dad would ask me if I wanted to go along with him and usually I would say "yes." Bar rooms were cool because there was always something new going on. The bar room across the street had a shuffle board game and they had this dog that would get up on the table, turn around, and shoot the weighted disc down the table with it's paw. At some bars my dad would roll the dice, at another he would try the punch board, and then there were darts and pinball machines; a variety of things to catch the watchful eye of a young boy. The best part was that my dad's friends would always buy me something to eat or drink; Slim Jims, Hershey bars, pretzels, and sodas. My mom would get mad because when we got home it was time for supper. Not to worry, I was a good eater, a habit I picked up from dad.

My dad enjoyed telling stories, and when he was talking you were expected to be extremely attentive. If you were distracted and your eyes wandered for a split second, you'd be on the receiving end of a backhand to your arm. This could happen quite a few times, and if my dad was engrossed in a long epic tale, you could end up with a black and blue mark. If my mother was the one hearing the story, it didn't take long before you heard mom yell, "Joe, knock it off," Sometimes when my brother and I are together, I'll do it to him, and then he starts doing it to me and we have one hell of a good laugh.

As I got older my friends and I would pack a lunch, fill our canteens, and grab our BB guns and head out for a day on the mountain above Tamaqua. My BB gun was special because the first time I laid eyes on that gun, it was showcased proudly in the window of Kutcher's Appliance Store on Broad Street. If you ever saw the movie, "A Christmas Story" that was what it was like for me. I was Ralphie, the kid who wanted the Red Rider BB Gun. I had to pass that store every day on my way to St. Jerome's School, and home again. Well, I concocted a plan and saved all my money to buy the gun. I went candy-less for a long time. Finally, I asked my big brother Guy if he would help me get the gun. We went downtown to the store, and he said, "give me your money."

We went inside and he told Mr. Kutcher he wanted to buy the BB gun in the window. It was a bit more than what I had, so Guy kicked in the rest. I finally had my own BB gun. The next phase of the plan was harder, how to tell my mom and dad about it. We walked in the door, me with the gun in hand, and immediately my dad said, "I told you that you couldn't have a BB gun."

My brother replied, "I think I'm old enough to have a BB gun dad." My dad said, "I know what's going on, and you'd better be with Joseph anytime he's shooting it." Guy said he would make sure I was careful with it. Wow, what a great brother.

We had some wild adventures up on the mountains, and I remember one day when we found the entrance to an old abandoned mine. Of course, as young, inquisitive lads, we decided we would go into the mine. Someone had a flashlight and aimed the beam at the end of the mine where we could see something shining. We thought we would go and discover what it was. Suddenly, somebody let out a bloodcurdling scream and lickety-split; we were all standing outside at the mine entrance. Looking back it was probably the best thing because some mines have air shafts that drop straight down; one of us could have fallen into one. That would have ruined the whole day.

We had an older cousin named Sonny who we didn't see often, but when he did come around he always held our interest. He was kind of a wild child, sort of like The Fonz. One day during the summer, he asked me if I wanted to go swimming with him and some friends at a swimming hole called "Paradise." I told him I had to check with my mom. She worked just up the street at a sewing factory so I went in and asked her and she told me "no." I went back to our house and grabbed my swimming suit off the line and told Sonny, "it's okay, let's go." Paradise was a bend in the Little Schuylkill River where the water swirled around, making a deep hole. On one side was a little beach area and across the river was a rock face that went up at an angle to form a cliff approximately fifty feet high. I remember seeing guys climb to the top and dive off into the river. You could never do that today because the water is not deep enough. I decided to swim to the other side where my cousin was and the swirling current pulled me under. I was able to surface once, then a second time. On the third time, Sonny grabbed me and pulled me out. I was scared shitless, and when I think back, I almost drowned in that river. I knew I'd be home before my mom got out of work and I hung my bathing suit back on the line. When she came home, she went out and checked my bathing suit only to find out that it was wet, my mom was pretty sharp like that. Well, she let me know she would tell my father that I disobeyed her and I knew the shit would hit the fan. My dad walloped me a good one and sent me to my room. That was about the extent of my punishment and I knew I deserved it. The next day, me and my parents were cool.

We did most of our swimming at the town pool where there were lifeguards. It was called The Bungalow, or as we referred to it, The Bungy. We would ride our bikes to the bungalow every day during the summer, unless it was a rainy day. The water for the pool came from a fresh spring up above it, so naturally the water was rather cool. We would spend all day there. My cousin Paul, Aunt

Gen's son, would never come out of the water, even when his lips were blue.

In the winter, the pool served as an ice skating rink. I hated the cold; even to this day I hate it. I keep threatening to move down south to a warmer climate, like my brother Guy, who had the good sense to move to North Carolina years ago.

When I was around the age of nine, my brother decided to join the Navy with some of his friends from high school. It was a depressing time for me, to see my brother going away, but it was also neat to tell my friends that Guy was in the United States Navy, protecting us. He was assigned as a radioman aboard the U.S.S. Independence, an aircraft carrier. Their ship took part in the Cuban Missile Crisis, and it was exciting watching it all unfold on the television. The world was on the brink of nuclear war at the time, so thankfully nothing came of it.

Growing up in the coal region could sometimes have its drawbacks. You see, everyone knew everyone back then. I recall one particular instance when I was out of the Army and working for Air Products and Chemicals in Allentown. I was on the afternoon shift and on the way home we would occasionally stop at a bar room or two for some drinks. We were getting into Tamaqua and it was late, and my friend, Sam, wanted to stop in a bar called Took One's. He said he was a regular there, so they would let him in after closing. He told me to go around into the alley on the side of the bar, and he would go into the bathroom, open the window, and help me climb in. Well, I did, and we enjoyed a few libations well into the night. That took place on a Friday night.

One might ask how the bar got its unusual moniker. My dad once explained it to me like this. "Back in those days when you were sitting at a bar and you wanted to buy someone a drink, you'd look at them and say 'took one' as opposed to 'have a drink on me' or 'let me buy you one.'" That's basically it in a nutshell.

I went to my parents' home that Sunday for dinner. My mother asked me, "What were you doing climbing into Took One's window at 2:00 AM on Friday?" I said, "holy shit mom, how do you know that?" She said a woman she worked with at the sewing factory lives in the next building, heard the commotion outside, and looked out to see her son, climbing in the window." My mom reminded me, "You can't get away with anything in this town without someone knowing about it." She was dead right.

THROUGH A YOUNG BOY'S EYES

Chapter 2

A.J.'s mother and I started getting concerned about him because he was coming around very slowly to speaking anything other than the usual "ma ma" and "da." We took him to the doctor and we were advised to make an appointment for him to be seen by specialists at Geisinger Medical Center in Danville. The doctors there gave him quite an extensive examination and concluded that A.J. just wasn't ready to talk yet. We were told that when he was ready, the snowball effect would come into play. Now keep in mind, he was just about four years old. Well, lo and behold, one day he just started, and from then on you could not shut him up. I think he got the gift of gab from his sister, Elizabeth.

I planted a peach tree in the backyard and it was doing quite well until A.J. and his friend decided to attack it one day. They were hacking away at it with some improvised swords and made a mess of it. I had to dig up the tree and plant a new one. This time I planted a Cortland apple tree which provided us with apples for many years to come. The woman next door would ask if she could pick some to make pies, and I would heartily agree. Her pies were quite delicious.

When A.J. was around five years of age his mother and I divorced; he and his sister stayed with their mom. Although we didn't see eye to eye, it was never a problem when I wanted to see my children. They moved to Jim Thorpe, Pennsylvania, into the house that was owned by a great aunt of their mother, Aunt Lizzy. I stayed in the house in Tamaqua. Weekends were usually the time I would make arrangements to pick up A.J. and Elizabeth to bring them over to be with me.

We did the usual things such as going to movies, parks, sporting events, visiting family and friends; but the one thing my children really enjoyed was going over to the Krell's house. They had a swimming pool that was an attraction in the summer. Their daughter, Dianne, would sit with Elizabeth and A.J. and tutor them. Elizabeth would become totally absorbed in it, but A.J. wasn't quite as fascinated. He'd be running around the yard chasing young Roy Krell and his friend Steve Wilson, while Donny Krell and I would be watching, taking in one of our favorite pastimes: drinking beer and eating fresh tomatoes and turnips from his garden. Sometimes there would be shots in between the beers and Donny would decide to sing a verse or two. He had some unusual songs in his repertoire, but one in particular sticks out. It went something like this: "Rye whiskey, rye whiskey, rye whiskey I cried, if I don't get rye whiskey, I think I will die. If the ocean was whiskey and I was a duck, I'd swim to the bottom, and never come up. Rye whiskey, rye whiskey, rye whiskey I cried, if I don't get rye whiskey I surely will die."

When the seasons changed and winter set in, we would move inside. The Krells had a Nintendo, so A.J. would involve himself in that, along with Roy, while Elizabeth would continue to be schooled by Dianne. It would seem that Dianne was instrumental in Elizabeth's learning that would later benefit her in high school and college. My children and I, would spend many memorable hours at the home of June and Donny Krell. They became, for me, my second mother and father, and I have been blessed to have them in my life. I am not embarrassed to say, "I love them."

One thing I can never forget is how the Krell family always invited me and my children over to share Christmas with them. Now keep in mind, Donny and June Krell had five children. Two of their daughters, Donna and June, were married with children of their own. That house, with all the gifts, and all the kids could get pretty crowded but they always made room in it for me and my children.

A.J. and I were even invited along on trips to the Krell's hunting camp in the Allegheny Mountains. I remember one particular time that Donny's brother Roy took along his young lad, also named Roy, and he made great company for A.J. Both boys took to one another and were pals the whole weekend. Young Roy made up a nickname for A.J. calling him Ajax the whole time. We took the boys down the mountain to the Big Pine River for some fishing, which they thoroughly enjoyed. They even spotted a river otter in the water. We went out spotting deer toward evening and even saw some turkeys. Then at night we'd sit around a big campfire and tell stories while the boys roasted marshmallows. The next day we went tubing down the river, with people sitting out by the riverbank just enjoying the outdoors. And no wonder; it was such a beautiful day. It was common to yell to them, say hello, or if I saw them drinking beer, to ask for one. Most would oblige and throw one out to me. It was a most memorable time in A.J.'s life and mine as well.

Donny Krell was like one of those things you find inside a washing machine: an agitator. I recall a time just after we moved to Penn Street in Tamaqua and I happened to be outside hanging some wash on the line. Suddenly I heard Donny Krell's voice, "Hey Charlie, take a look at Joe Baddick over there."

Then I heard Charlie Myers' reply, "Oh boy, there goes the neighborhood."

Then Donny once again, "How do you get your whites so white Joey Baby?"

Then Charlie, "What kind of laundry detergent do you use; your clothes look so bright?" The two magpies kept giving me the business until I went into the house. You could always count on a good ribbing from those two.

I had been involved in painting the outside of our house for weeks, and my project was near its end. I had removed the rain gutters and painted them, and I left them on a lower roof at the rear of the house. My plan was to come home from work, change, and put the gutters back up so I would be finished with my project. Well, when I went out back, the gutters weren't there. I had a stinking suspicion who the culprit was. As I looked around, my other neighbor, Mr. Rogers, asked me if something was wrong. I told him about the gutters and he said, "Well, I'm not sure where they are, but you might want to ask Donny." So, my suspicions were correct. I shot over to Donny's house and knocked on the door. His wife, June, answered the door. I told her what happened and she said she didn't know anything about my gutters, but I was welcome to look around. June Krell was the type of person that would never, ever, tell a lie, so I believed her. I started to look around their house, under the deck, the rear of the house, up by the shed, along the fence, but my search was fruitless. Just then, Donny came home and, with my blood pressure going off the charts, I said, "you son of a bitch, where's my rain gutters?" He just smiled and said, "hold on Joey Baby, calm down before you explode. Did you look everywhere?" I replied, "Yeah, I looked everywhere, now where the hell are they?" Donny said, "Did ya happen to look in the garden?" Oh man, I was fumin', I went over to the garden, and there, between the rows of tomato plants, lay my rain gutters.

Then I hear, "I ain't sayin' I took them, but I saw someone putting something in the garden earlier." I took them over and installed them and when I was finished, there was Donny with two beers. I finally calmed down and realized how funny it was.

Another time I was grilling outside and I had put potatoes, wrapped in tin foil, on the grill. I came outside later on and, lo and behold, the potatoes were missing in action. Right away, I ran over to Donny's house to find the missing spuds. He said he didn't do it. I asked him who did. He said his son Roy and his buddy Steve Wilson needed some potatoes for a camping trip they were going on, and maybe they had them. I went outside and asked Roy about the potatoes, and he immediately said, "My dad told us to do it." Oh, what a surprise that was. That guy was the King of Pranks, but it was fun.

Donny taught me everything I know about the upkeep of a house, from putting on a new roof, to fixing plumbing leaks, installing tile ceilings, repairing a furnace, doing cement work, and many other needful things. He helped me fix my car many times, and taught me to become a rather adept wing shooter with a shotgun. This man taught me things one cannot learn in a college or university. One very important lesson I learned from Donny was to mind your own business and not gossip about other people.

In earlier years, my dad and Donny Krell worked together at the #14 colliery just outside of town. The colliery was a building near the coal mining area that sized the coal stripped from the hillsides. Huge loaders dumped the coal at the top and different size screens separated the coal as it fell through.

Donny told me a story once about their one foreman, Chatty Gould, who owned a bar in Lansford. He would always go to the wash shanty and clean up, put on fresh clothes, and leave work early so he could get to his bar. One day my dad was on the upper floor and Donny could hear him making some noise so he went up to take a look. There was my dad making some sort of a platform near an open door. Donny didn't think much of it and went back downstairs. Later on my dad called Donny to come upstairs and help him. He asked my dad what he wanted and my dad told him he needed help getting a fifty five gallon drum over to the doorway. Donny looked into the drum and it was filled about halfway with oil. He asked my dad why he was doing this and my dad told him not to worry about it and just give him a hand. They rolled the fifty five gallon drum to the edge of the doorway and my dad said they would have to wait a few minutes. A little while later, my dad pointed to Chatty Gould who was coming down the path from the wash shanty. My dad instructed Donny to help him tilt the drum on end and when Chatty Gould got underneath the doorway, they dumped the oil on top of him. Donny said, "When the oil hit Chatty Gould, it knocked him flat on his ass."

Then my dad took a forty pound bag of oil dry and dumped it down on top of poor Chatty. Well, Chatty Gould got to his feet, looked up, and started yelling, "Josey Baddick, I'll fire you for this, I'll fire you, you son of a bitch." My dad never did get fired and Donny never tired of telling the story of how he and my dad tarred and feathered ole' Chatty Gould.

Chatty Gould would also have some of the men take his car and wash it because he would go out dancing on a Friday night. One time he sent my dad and another man to wash his car and my dad didn't come back with his car for hours. That was the last time my dad was sent along to wash the car.

Another story Donny Krell told me was about the time he had his foot broken at the mine. The doctor had cast his foot and Donny always managed to mess up the cast, so he had to return to the doctor to have it recast on more than one occasion. After about four visits, the doctor told Donny that would be the last time he would give him a new cast. Anyway, Donny was working at the #14 colliery and took on the job of riding on the back of the train that would haul away the coal to be dumped. The only way the engineer would know the coal was dumped and the man on the back was ready to go would be for the man on the back to wave his lantern. Well, with Donny's foot in a cast, he was moving slow, and the engineer took off without him. When the train got back, my dad noticed Donny wasn't on the back. He asked the engineer where Donny was and he told my dad he didn't know. At that, my dad pulled the rope that stopped all activity at the colliery. Work came to a screeching halt. The foreman came out and wanted to know who pulled the rope, and my dad told him he did, because they couldn't find Donny Krell.

When they finally got to Donny they asked him what happened. He said he wasn't sure, he didn't remember if he waved the lantern or not. He said he didn't want to get anybody in trouble.

Donny Krell said my dad pulled the rope on more than one occasion. My dad was a strictly, by the book, union man. Anytime there was a rule being violated or a safety concern, my dad would pull the rope. Donny said my dad got into it more than once with the foreman. One time, the foreman came out, asked why the rope was pulled, and not thinking it to be a big deal, attempted to reach for the rope to restart production, and my dad said, "you touch that rope and I'll knock your block off." Donny said the foreman used good judgment and walked away. He said back in those days all the guys stuck together, and if there was a serious reason, they could shut production down as long as they wanted.

If you ever want to experience what it was like to be a miner, I would highly recommend a visit to the Pioneer Tunnel Coal Mine, located in Ashland, Pennsylvania. The tour takes you inside a real coal mine by way of a tram. Once inside the mine, you exit the tram and a guide walks you through areas that were at one time, in use, and where men did back breaking work to earn a living.

I had a girlfriend named Kathy who moved in with me, along with her two sons, Erik and T.J. When A.J. was over visiting, the boys could become a handful. As normal boys, they would have their differences, but for the most part they got along quite well. I remember in the winter, I would make a sort of toboggan run coming down the yard for the boys to use. At the bottom, by the house, I would place two plastic garbage cans and pile snow around them because there were two small windows there. I would get the three boys at the top of the yard where they would sit, all three of them, on one of those hard plastic sheets, and then give them a push. They would hit the garbage cans and roll over laughing like banshees. We would do this over and over again, until they wore me out. I also had a German shorthaired pointer named Luke. Erik named him after Luke Skywalker, since Star Wars was a huge hit at that time. Luke would join in the festivities chasing the boys up and down the yard. Luke was my hunting dog, and a few years later A.J. would start hunting and join me and Luke in the field on many good outings. There was this one day that I was watching T.J. and I had to go out to a local store called Jamesway. I had T.J. in the back seat and he was eating Reese's Pieces. As I was pulling into the parking lot, T.J. started to cry. I asked him what was wrong and he replied, "I got a Reese's Pieces stuck in my nose." I slammed the brakes on and said, "holy shit." I put the car in park and turned around to check him out. I tilted his head back, and lo and behold, I had an orange Reese's Pieces staring me in the face. I took the keys out of the ignition and used the car key to pop it out of his nose.

There's just something about car keys and me. One time we went to a Tamaqua basketball game, and Kathy's sister, Kelly, was a cheerleader. We went with Kathy's mom and A.J. was along. I drove her mom's car and after the game we went out to the car, it was a very cold night. Her mom put the key in the door lock to open the car and the key broke off. I asked if she had another one and she replied, "No." Right away, panic set in. "Oh my God, it's so cold, we're gonna freeze" said one of the women. I managed to pick the broken piece of key out of the door lock and save it. Then I went to work on getting us in the car. I borrowed a coat hanger and slipped it into the window to pop the lock open. Now we were inside the car and someone asked, "how are we gonna start the car?" I thought a minute and asked if there was a hammer or something in the car. Kathy found a screw driver and I said, "That will work." I put the broken piece of the key in the ignition and next went the top half of the key. I whacked it with the handle of the screw driver a few times to seat it and then turned the ignition. The car started and we managed to avert a catastrophe. A.J. said, "I knew you'd think of something dad." Of course, Kathy's mom never needed to carry a key around with her from that day on, to start her car. After about two years, Kathy and I parted ways, but we shared many good times, and she was a very special chapter in my life.

My Uncle Frank - my dad's brother - had been a hunter and fisherman all his life. He had bird dogs that he would run in field trials. His house was a place I loved to visit. There were ribbons all around that his dogs won. He had custom made fly rods and up on the top floor he kept all his guns. He had Japanese rifles from the war along with a Jap flag. He also had German binoculars and a German pistol. The Japanese stuff he got from his brother Eddie who served in the Pacific Theater, and the German stuff was from his brother-in-law who was in the European Theater. He also had reloading equipment for his rifles and shotguns that he showed me how to work. His wife, Rose, was as avid a hunter and fisherman as he was. My Aunt Rose would go to the trap shoots with him and they say she could outshoot my Uncle Frank by hitting twenty five out of twenty five clay birds.

Uncle Frank was a personal friend of Johnny Weismuller, the guy who played Tarzan in the first movies. Johnny was an Olympic swimmer and he would travel around the country putting on swimming exhibitions. When he was in our area he would look up

Uncle Frank and they would head over to Lake Hauto, between Tamaqua and Nesquehoning, where they would swim the length of the lake a few times before heading home. To this day, my Aunt Eleanor Paslawsky has a book autographed by Johnny Weismuller that was my uncle Frank's. It reads, "To my good friend, Frank Baddick, from Johnny Weismuller."

Uncle Frank used to take me and A.J. fishing at a place called Shikellamy Trout Hatchery near Bethal, Pa. It was a great place for youngsters to fish because no matter what type of bait you put on the hook, the fish would bite. It was a thrill for A.J. and he caught a lot of fish. They would clean your fish for a small fee and we would go home and fry them up in a pan for supper. There's just something special about eating freshly caught trout. My Uncle Frank was also very active with the Little Lehigh Trout Hatchery near Allentown, Pa.

One thing that stood out about A.J. was his ability to remember things; many times, things the rest of us had forgotten. I recall a time that we were riding in the car and A.J. came out with, "that's the house that Casey went to." Casey was our first dog, an Irish setter. There were other instances too, many of them, that would amaze us about A.J. He remembered everything. We'd be trying to think of a movie we saw or a TV show and A.J. would blurt it out. If you took A.J. anywhere and they had arcade games he would always be interested in the racing games. He loved games where you sat in a car or on a motorcycle. He became pretty good at it too. There is a place a few miles out in the country from Tamaqua called Heisler's. It was a dairy, and the owner had put in a miniature golf course, an ice cream bar, an arcade, a golf ball driving range and a waffle bar. A.J. always liked when I took him there because they had some of those car and motorcycle games, not to mention the area's best ice cream. One time Sheila and I were taking A.J. to the movies and the theater had four screens, so when we got there we looked at what was playing and we told A.J. he could pick. He decided on Ernest Goes to Camp. When we came out of the movie theatre and A.J. couldn't hear, Sheila made it very clear that I was never to take her to a stupid movie like that again. I replied, "Yes dear."

I went over to pick up Elizabeth and A.J. one day and all I could say upon seeing my son was, "what the heck happened to you?" Before A.J. could respond, his sister replied, "He decided to cut his own hair, dad." Well, he was quite a sight. One side of his head was shaved almost clean and at the most unusual, uneven angle, as if the Blind Barber of Seville had him in his chair. All I could do was laugh and tell him, "thank God son, it will grow back." I think he attempted that little fiasco because some football hero of his had a new do.

A.J. and I took a trip to visit an old Army buddy of mine by the name of Chuck Lumley, who lived in Hampton, Virginia. Chuck and I spent many hours playing handball and a card game called spades while we were stationed at Ft. Bragg, NC. When we arrived, Chuck was working part time at the local police station. He said he would be done in a couple of hours so A.J. and I took in a movie. We went to see "Days of Thunder" with Tom Cruise. It was a movie about racing and A.J. loved it.

The next day Chuck took us to an all-you-can-eat seafood restaurant. I love seafood, but A.J. kept right up with me. We went to see Ft. Eustis, where Chuck retired from. There, they have the Transportation Museum which is devoted to the history of military transportation. We also stopped to see Ft. Monroe, which protected to entrance to Hampton Roads. A.J. learned that Jefferson Davis was the President of the Confederacy during the Civil War and was held captive there for two years. We viewed his prison cell and some of his personal memorabilia which was very interesting. As we were leaving we noticed something coming closer out in the water and it turned out to be a submarine, which was quite exciting, especially for A.J.

We later said goodbye to Chuck and headed north. We ended up in Wildwood, New Jersey and decided to get a room for the night. While we were checking in, the front desk clerk told us it was our lucky day. We asked why and he said there was an all female musical group staying there called "The Bangles." A.J.'s eyes lit up like the Fourth of July. Well, we never did get to see the Bangles, but we had a great time in Wildwood anyway. A.J. wanted to get on a ride that took you way up and stopped, then released you and did it again, only in reverse. After he got off the ride he told me he would never get on it again. That must have been some ride, and he decided to jump out of airplanes. Go figure. We came home the next day; it was a memorable trip for the both of us.

A.J. took an interest in baseball around the age of eight and started playing in the Jim Thorpe League. We went over to watch him play and on this one particular day he decided he would be the catcher, (I guess because nobody else wanted the job). He was quite amusing because every couple of pitches the coach would have to stop the game so A.J. could readjust his equipment. His shin guards kept falling down because they were made for a larger player. He insisted he wanted to continue catching and the coach let him, but it sure was a long game. One thing about my son, he was persistent. We had some good laughs at his expense that day.

I bought A.J. a .22 caliber rifle, a single shot, his first real gun. I taught him all the basics of shooting along with gun handling and safety. We took it over to show Donny Krell, who at the time was doing a lot of wood burning projects. He asked if we wanted to put A.J.'s name on the gun and we told him yes. He wood burned into the stock, "A.J. Baddick" 1988. He was thrilled with it and I still have the gun to this day. I suppose it will be handed down to someone in the family, for safe keeping.

I remember taking A.J. to the Bloomsburg Fairgrounds to see a monster truck competition. We had a blast and A.J. really enjoyed seeing all the monster trucks. Back then, Gravedigger was one of the trucks and it is still very popular today. I watch the monster trucks on the television and they have come a long way. It's still exciting to watch.

COMING OF AGE

Chapter 3

Around this time I met my future wife, Sheila; A.J. was about thirteen years old. Sheila rented a condo in Ocean City, Maryland each summer, so she invited us along. I noticed an advertisement for a Polish Festival being held in Bucks County and the hostess was a lady I greatly admired from my childhood. Her name was Sally Starr; that was her television name. She hosted a show called Popeye Theater and each day I would run home from school to see her dressed in her cowgirl outfit. I would give her a kiss and my mother would yell at me that she just cleaned the TV screen. Sally would tell stories and show a Three Stooges episode. Anyway, Sheila said we could stop by the festival on our way to the beach and I told her that would be great. When we arrived we walked around for awhile and then bought a bottle of wine and some food to enjoy. As we sat there, Sally, or as she was better known, Our Gal Sal, stepped out and began talking to the crowd. She asked if any of her baby boomers were in the audience. I immediately raised my hand and she asked, "Where are you from sir?" I said, "Tamaqua," to which she replied, "Ah, the coal region. Tamaqua, Mahanoy City, Shenandoah. I always enjoyed that area of Pennsylvania." Later on I asked her if we could get a picture with her and she graciously complied with my request. I was lucky enough to get a photo op with Sally Starr; and we cherish it to this day. Thanks to my dear wife, Sheila, I was able to relive some of my childhood memories and include A.J. among them.

We left the festival and headed for the beach in Ocean City, Maryland. I remember arriving and it was raining cats and dogs, so after we checked in, we took A.J. to the movies. The next day the sun was out and we spent most of the next few days on the beach. Sheila's daughter, Tyna and her friend were also with us. One evening we decided to go out to eat at a place called Harpoon Hanna's. While we were eating Tyna made a remark about our busboy being cute and A.J. thought he would be of assistance. So when the busboy came back to our table, A.J. told him, "My sister thinks you're hot." Well, both Tyna and the young man turned beet red with him dropping a dish and her sliding under the table. We all had a good laugh that night but A.J. paid for it. A few days later A.J. was talking to some girls from Baltimore and Tyna told them all about A.J. and how much he liked them. From that day on A.J. couldn't get rid of them. After we went home they even wrote to him.

Our condo was high up and I had brought along binoculars, so A.J. and I went out on the balcony to check things out. I happened to be using the binoculars and Sheila came out and asked what I was looking at. I said,

"Ah, I'm looking for boats out on the ocean." With that, my son says, "and girls on the beach." That didn't go over too well with Sheila. Anyway, it turned out to be a great vacation and A.J. sure enjoyed himself.

This was around the time I decided to marry Sheila, and on November 29, 1991, I made her my wife. I'm not so sure we picked a good day to be wed because it was Black Friday. Who the hell gets married on Black Friday?

We have a huge marriage certificate hanging on the wall which reads: "Sheila and Joseph, who have chosen each other out of all the species, with the design to be each other's mutual comfort and entertainment, have, in that action, bound themselves to be good humored, affable, discreet, forgiving, patient, and joyful, with respect to each other's frailties, and perfections, to the end of their lives. - Addison." The witness signatures on this certificate are Andrew J. Baddick and Tyna Jones. Sheila chose her daughter as her Maid of Honor and I chose A.J. to be my Best Man, and he sure turned out to be the best man I've ever known. Andrew looked so handsome all dressed up, and he was a happy guy standing up for his dad. He really enjoyed himself.

In 1995, my daughter, Elizabeth, graduated from East Stroudsburg University. Sheila and I were scheduled to go, once again, to Ocean City, Maryland. We decided we would attend Elizabeth's graduation ceremony, and from there, head directly to O.C. Until that time, I had never attended a university graduation. As the graduates entered the hall, according to their respective status, I eagerly awaited the nursing program, of which Elizabeth was a part. I became totally wrapped up in the moment. When the nursing graduates entered the hall, I was so proud, and for some odd reason, became teary eyed. My beautiful daughter was graduating from East Stroudsburg University, with a B.S. Degree in Nursing. This was a momentous occasion. She has never ceased to amaze me. She has gone on to hold some first rate jobs, and there have been times when I go back and think about her and Dianne Krell hammering away at the school work.

There was an incident that A.J. was involved in one summer in Jim Thorpe that had dire consequences. Andrew and some of his buddies went down to the Lehigh River, and started goofing around, as most boys will do. It was a warm day, so A.J. decided he would jump in the river to cool off with a swim. Another boy told A.J., "If you can go in for a swim, so can I." The young lad was swept away with the current only to be found hours later, downstream, drowned. The town of Jim Thorpe would live with a terrible tragedy that day, and for many days to come. Here we have another example of an event in my son's life that would become part of his destiny. I think this episode troubled my son for quite awhile, but it's strange, it never kept him away from the water. Even after witnessing this terrible event, A.J. was always comfortable around water.

A.J. had always had a fascination with the outdoors and hunting, I suppose, since that was a big part of my life. I was a hunter since I was old enough to get a license. It's funny, but neither my dad nor my older brother were hunters. Somehow I just decided that I wanted to hunt. Luckily I had my Uncle Frank - my dad's brother - who had bird dogs and did quite a bit of hunting himself. Uncle

Frank took me out hunting pheasants with his dogs on many occasions. I also had my cousin, Rich Campbell, who was always willing to teach me about hunting - especially archery hunting - which became my all time favorite.

Weekends at my house were very special for A.J. when hunting season was in. I'd pick him up on a Friday after work and all he talked about was going out hunting the next morning. A.J. had a cassette tape by an artist named Jude Cole, and one of his songs was, "Start the Car." Every time we were going somewhere in the car, especially hunting, A.J. would tell me to play that song, and then he would say, "turn it up dad." So, I would humor him and turn it up loud, and a big smile would appear on A.J.'s face.

One thing about him was that, when I was teaching him something, he was all ears. He paid strict attention to what I was saying and then applied it in the field. Now I know people who were familiar with my son would find this hard to believe, but when we would be out archery hunting, he was quiet as a mouse. A.J. became quite an accomplished and successful hunter.

On one particular outing, we were walking into the back end of Tuscarora State Park to archery hunt, and it was at that time of the morning when it was just starting to get light out and you can't really see clear yet. A.J. whispered to me, "Dad, what's that up ahead on the path?" I looked, straining my eyes, and said, "It's just a bush." My son replied, "Ah dad, the bush just moved." So we moved up and as we get closer I'm looking at a black bear, and he's looking at us. So I ask politely, "okay Yogi, are you gonna move or are we?" At the sound of my voice, the bear took off running into a field, with the sound of bushes and small trees breaking. Right after he ran off, another bear came tearing across the path and followed the first one. A.J. thought it was great, and I have to admit, I was a bit excited myself.

We would get to our spot and I would put A.J. near some laurel bushes for cover, and then I would get up in a tree with my stand not too far from him. I would make sure I could see him. I told him that when I saw deer coming in I would whistle and he would know to get ready. I just loved watching my son at that point because he was on his own and showing me what he learned. There was a lot of trial and error in the first few years but the experience was good for him and he learned from his mistakes.

I did a lot of spotting around for deer signs and one day I found an area where I knew a buck was visiting, so I decided we would hunt there the upcoming weekend. We went to the spot, I put out some scent, and we both went up trees on either side of it. I decided to use a new technique this time and brought along a set of antlers. If you rattle them together a buck will think his territory is being trespassed upon and come to investigate. Well, sure as shootin', after a while, old Mr. Buck came up the bank from down below where it's thick with laurel bushes. He was a beautiful six pointer and wanted to know what all the commotion was about. I looked over at A.J. and nodded for him to take the shot. He waited for the right moment, when the deer had his nose down, pulled his bow back, and fired. Now I'm thinking, all that work and he missed. The arrow hit just under the buck and stuck in the ground. He looked at me, raised his hands in the air, and all I could do was smile. We waited awhile, and then got out of our stands. I asked A.J., "What the heck happened son?" His reply was, "I guess I got buck fever." That's the feeling you get when the deer is coming in and your whole body shakes from the excitement, the adrenaline is really pumping. We sure had some good laughs over it at A.J.'s expense. However, in the following years A.J. would learn to control his feelings and shoot a number of deer with his bow.

On another archery hunt we were accompanied by my cousin Rich, and again, we were at Tuscarora Park. We found a good spot for A.J. and then I found a tree to climb. Rich hunted on the ground so he went to find a spot for himself. I had just purchased a new climbing tree stand called a Loggy Bayou. It had rained the night before and the trees were wet. I started to climb the tree and I was up about fifteen feet when I decided one more good pull would put me up where I needed to be. I made the mistake of reaching too high and got on my toes, a huge mistake, because the band that wraps around the tree let go and I experienced the fastest elevator ride down, ever.

Well, the stand stopped about two feet from the ground, my knees buckled, and I feel sideways off the stand. I lay on the ground with my feet still under the toe bar on the stand. Rich came over and said, "I was watching you climb the tree and I heard a noise, so I looked away to see if it was deer, and when I looked back, you were gone. I said, "Well, this is where I went to." A.J. came running over and said he saw me going down the tree and asked if I was okay. I said, "I guess so, let me get up and we'll see."

I walked around and seemed to be alright. I finished hunting that day on the ground. The next day A.J. and I went to a sporting goods store and I bought myself a safety harness, something I hadn't used for many years. I also bought a hand climber that day.

A.J. also enjoyed hunting with the dog for birds. Luke would point the pheasants for us and I would tell A.J. to walk toward the point and suddenly a bird would take wing. He would shoot a few birds with Luke's help, but many more got away on him. We were out shooting groundhogs with Donny Krell one time and there was a fence on the farm that we had to get past. I wasn't paying attention to A.J. and I heard him let out a yell. When I turned around he was by the fence and jumping around. Seems the fence turned out to be electric and he had the misfortune of touching it. Oh well, live and learn. We had some laughs with that incident. One time A.J. was out hunting with his rifle and he shot a coyote. He was a pretty darn good hunter. Some of my fondest memories of my son were the times we spent together in the outdoors.

We ate a lot of the game we shot. A.J. loved deer meat and I would make steaks and chops for him. Man, could he eat. I guess we shouldn't have been surprised since my dad and I were such big eaters. They say my dad would take his lunch in a brown shopping bag to work. His buddies would say, "I wonder what's in Josey's mystery bag today." They said my dad had a cast iron stomach, and I believe it. I did pretty good myself. The first time I ever had buffalo wings, I ate sixty four of them. More recently I ate twelve dozen oysters, half a pound of shrimp, and a crab cake, then washed it all down with four beers. Yep, us Baddick's can eat. One of A.J.'s favorite things was eating pickles and my dad's hot balonies. My dad always made sure he had pickles and hot baloney at his house when A.J. came over to visit. He liked the big kosher dill type pickles.

The area around Jim Thorpe was big on river rafting since the Lehigh River split the town in half. There was a rafting center not far from where A.J. lived and he developed an interest in kayaking. When rafting trips went down the river, there would be river guides in kayaks following them to make sure the trips were safe. I was told that A.J. became so proficient at kayaking that he could have been an instructor. He used to work as a guide on the river and he loved it. He told me that he had a cassette tape I needed to hear. It just so happened that A.J. guided a group of people from Michigan down the river, and they happened to be friends of Ted Nugent. For those of you not familiar with him, he is a musician who started out playing with The Amboy Dukes, then went solo. He has a radio show in Michigan and he is an avid hunter, especially with the bow. It's no wonder he was A.J.'s idol. Well, this cassette tape was sent to A.J. from Ted Nugent's radio show. On it, Nugent explains how some friends of his were in Jim Thorpe, Pennsylvania, on a rafting trip down the Lehigh River, and their guide was one A.J. Baddick, who treated them so well he had to give him kudos for a job well done. A.J. was really thrilled to have received that cassette tape from his idol, Ted Nugent.

This was around the time A.J. was attending Jim Thorpe High School. He had an interest in football and wrestling. He was never really great at either one but he enjoyed it and that was all that mattered. A.J. had some close friends, but none closer than Kevin Trice. They were the same age and, I was told, they were like brothers. Once again, tragedy would strike the town of Jim Thorpe. Kevin and Nancy Trice would lose their son to a horrible accident. It was the first day of February, 1997. Kevin went over to the house of a girlfriend, Carrie Hydro, along with some other friends. It was cold that day and a coal stove was burning for warmth. Sometime during the evening carbon monoxide fumes filled the house. One of the boys awoke and felt that something was terribly wrong. He was able to get the others awake and outside but Kevin Trice would not awake from his deep sleep; he was dead. Five others received treatment due to the carbon monoxide fumes.

Kevin played football for Marian High School, wearing the number 28, and Coach Stan Dick said Kevin had a lot of potential to further his football career. Coincidentally, Kevin was born at Ft. Benning, GA. That is where A.J. took jump training to become a paratrooper. These two boys were friends with a common bond.

This was a very emotional time for A.J. and there was a noticeable change in his personality. He didn't seem to have the zest for life that he did before Kevin's death. A.J. finally graduated high school and started working. He moved from one job to another and started to drink quite a bit. He was in a few accidents and managed to wreck two vehicles, his own and no one else's, thank God. A.J. was also getting into a lot of fights. It was quite evident that A.J. was in a slump. This went on for awhile and we became very concerned, no one more than his sister,

Elizabeth. She would call me almost on the verge of tears saying her brother was drinking way too much and he was going to kill someone, driving drunk, or himself. I explained to her that he was going to do what he felt he needed to do but that I would talk to him. When we did talk A.J. mentioned to me that he was considering going into the army. I told him I thought that was a good idea and to let me know if he became serious about it.

A short time later A.J. told me he had stopped to see a recruiter and they discussed him being available to go to Harrisburg to the main recruitment office. He asked me if I would go along and I said I would be glad to. The day we went A.J. was somewhat excited so I took him off to the side and explained to him that he shouldn't jump at the first thing they offered him, such as infantry, cook, etc. I told A.J. to ask what other options were available to him. He came out of the office and told me he accepted an available slot as a cook. I guess the look in my eyes told him the whole way I felt and he immediately laughed and said he was just fooling. I made a fist and shook it at him and asked, "So just what did you sign up for?" A.J. said he remembered what I had told him, and the only slots available were cook and infantry, so he told the recruiter he would wait and see what else opened up. I told A.J. I was so glad he took my advice. I spoke with the sergeant and told him to give A.J. a call if some other slots opened up. We went back home and I told A.J. to be patient and things would work out for him.

A few weeks passed and one night around two o'clock in the morning I would receive another phone call that all parents dread. My son was calling to tell me goodbye, he was going to kill himself. I immediately started to recall all the training I had received dealing with suicide as a corrections officer over the years. I knew that if a person was serious about committing the act they usually don't announce it, and if they do turn to someone, it's probably a cry for help. I asked A.J. why? He said life sucked and he missed his friend Kevin and nothing was working out for him. I asked him if he realized all the people that would be hurt if he followed through with this: me and Sheila, his mom and sister, his gram and pap and all his friends. He said he didn't want to hurt anyone but he was hurting real bad. I kept talking to him and tried to keep him on the phone but after about twenty minutes he told me goodbye and if I didn't hear from him again, he loved me, then hung up the phone. I was so crazy; I didn't know what to do next. I called his mom and asked if he called her and she said he had and that she called the police about him. I started to pray to the Blessed Mother like never before. She had always helped me in my time of need and this was no exception. I knew there was nowhere I could go because I didn't even know where A.J. was; he wouldn't tell me. I decided to just pray and pray and pray. Finally, after what seemed an eternity, the phone rang and I was petrified. I was so scared to answer it but I knew I must. It was A.J.'s mom and she said the police found him and he had a loaded rifle in his truck. They took him to the Lehighton hospital to the psychiatric unit. By now it was getting light out and it was the most glorious light I can ever remember. My son was alive. I went to the hospital to see him and there I met an aide whose name was Kevin Duke. I said to him, "you look very familiar, do you know me?" He said,

"Joe Baddick, didn't you work at the Atlas Powder Company?" "Yes, I did, that's where I know you from, nice to see you again." I asked how A.J. was doing and Kevin told me he was very depressed and needed professional help. Kevin showed me to A.J.'s room and when I entered and saw him, lying in the bed, I couldn't believe it was my son. He clearly had been through hell and he just laid there, looking totally out of it. I put my arm around him and gave him a kiss, but he was emotionless. I asked how he was and he just shrugged his shoulders. We started to talk but it was basically a one-sided conversation. I stayed about an hour and told A.J. I would be back the next day with some hunting magazines for him. As I left, Kevin came over and said he would take good care of my son. I thanked him and left. My mind was a blur as I drove home. I just couldn't believe that was my son in the hospital, he had such a zest for life and now it was if the life had been drained out of him. What was I to do?

After a few days A.J. started looking a little better. He cleaned himself up and was more talkative. I got a phone call from his mom and she said the Army recruiter was looking for him. She told him A.J. had gone away on a trip to see some friends. Now I'm thinking, "oh boy, A.J. really blew it; the army won't accept him with this on his record." I went to the hospital and looked up Kevin. I asked what we could do. He said I would need to talk to Dr. Paschal. I said, "Dr. who?" He repeated, "Dr. Paschal." I said I knew a Dr. Paschal from my days working at the State Correctional Institution in Frackville. Kevin said, "yes, that's him, he does some work there in the mental health unit."

I told A.J. about the recruiter looking for him and that I was going to talk to Dr. Paschal to see if he could help us out. I did, and Dr. Paschal remembered me and explained that he could sign A.J. out of the hospital under my supervision. I asked the doc if there would be a problem with this on his record and he said no one would know because of the privacy laws.

I then had a thought about the Jim Thorpe police, since they were the ones who found A.J. that night. I called the chief and told him I would be taking A.J. to see the recruiter and asked what he could do to help. He told me that over the last few years A.J. had been a thorn in his side and if expunging his record would get him in the Army and out of town, we could count on him.

Everything seemed to be in order for us to go see the recruiter. I phoned the recruiter and told him I was able to get in touch with my son and we would come to Harrisburg to see him. When we got there A.J. asked me if he should hold out if there were no new slots open and I told him to do what he thought was best for him. When he came out he told me he wanted to sign up for the infantry. It wasn't my first choice for my son but considering the direction his life was headed in, I figured that was better than where he was now, so I said it was fine with me and we went into the recruiter's office, and A.J. signed up for the infantry. What the heck, it wouldn't be that bad; after all, I was in the infantry myself, the airborne infantry. We were told to stick around for a while because there were other recruits there and they would all be sworn in that day. A.J. and I talked and I told him I thought he was doing the right thing and he said, "Thanks dad."

All the recruits, about twenty of them, were ushered into a room for the oath of enlistment ceremony. The sergeant came over to me and said I could stand in the back of the room and observe. The recruits were called to attention, and as I looked at them I noticed that A.J. stood straight as a flagpole, shoulders back, hands at his side, like he had been doing it all his life. None of the others looked as good as my son did. I was so proud of A.J.; he was taking a huge step forward in his life. When the swearing in was over he turned to leave the room and had a big, shit-eatin' grin on his face. There was a tremendous change from the person I saw lying in the hospital bed, to the young man now standing before me.

On the ride home we spoke of many things but one thing I remember is telling A.J. what to expect when he got to basic training. I told him to be prepared for a lot of bullshit, but to take it all with a grain of salt. I explained to him that most of it was a game, a mind game, and he needed to know how to play it. I told him to listen closely to everything his instructors had to say and obey them without question. If they told him to do pushups, he should ask how many, and do an extra one. I told him to keep a smile on his face and not let the dumb shit get to him. He told me he understood, and he really did. He would prove it in the weeks to come.

The night before A.J. left for basic training, he called his sister at approximately 3:00 A.M. and told her he was on his way over to her house. Elizabeth couldn't imagine what this was all about but she went downstairs and waited by the door for her brother. Much to her surprise, A.J. arrived at the front door with a cat in his arm, asking her to keep the cat for him while he was away. Elizabeth asked him whose cat it was and A.J. replied, "It's my cat." His sister said, "You don't have a cat." He replied, "It is my cat, his name is Lucky." Again, his sister said, "it's not yours, you don't have a cat." A.J., in an obviously inebriated state, replied, "Oh Lucky, who loves daddy?" Elizabeth reminded him one more time that he didn't have a cat, while noticing that her cat was doing quite a bit of hissing. A.J. repeated, "Oh Lucky, Lucky, Lucky, who loves daddy, who loves daddy?" Elizabeth told her brother that there was no way in hell she would keep the cat. With that he stormed off. Elizabeth's husband, Shack, asked her, "What makes that boy tick?" It became a family thing whenever A.J. was around and he did something silly, Shack would say, "What makes that boy tick?"

Just before Christmas in 2008, there was a commercial running on the television for a stuffed dog that our granddaughter wanted, and his name was Lucky. Andi Rose told her mom and dad she wanted it. They looked at each other and decided, okay, they needed to get that for her because of Uncle A.J. Funny how things happen like that.

MEMOIRS

Chapter 4

It was October of 1999, and A.J. was on his way to basic training at Ft. Benning, Georgia. He would take both basic training and infantry school training there. I was going through some of the letters he wrote home and thought I would include parts of them, in his own words, into the book. Some include A.J.'s wit and some are quite profound.

"6 October, 1999. Dear Dad & Sheila, I'm doing fine here so far. The weather is great, about 80 degrees in the afternoon, but at night it gets very cold.

Everybody in my barracks is sick from the shots they gave us. Today, we're still processing but it is lunch time so I figured I'd write because I can't hold any chow down. Those vitamins that you got for me, I had to throw away. As soon as I got here they opened our bags and dumped them upside down and frisked us. My one friend is really cool, he keeps bringing me orange juice in my canteen and oranges for vitamin C. Coming back from processing I walked by a recruiter liason room and figured I'd go talk to him about going airborne. I told him you were in the 82nd and Uncle Eddie was in the 11th Airborne, and I would like to keep up the family tradition. He said I would have to talk to this one drill sergeant and ask him if he would refer me. If he does that means I will have an 82nd contract. Did Tyna and Rick come home from South Carolina yet? How is the baby (Kaitlyn) doing? You will have to send me a picture. Love ya, A.J. OXOXOX"

On 13 October, 1999, A.J. wrote:

"Well, I finally got to basic and it is my second day here. They loaded us up in horse trailers and brought us here. The drill sergeants were screaming at us, making us line up and hold our duffle bags that weighed about 100 lbs., and our personal bags, in each hand without putting them down. If you set them down to take a rest, you had to do pushups, then get up and hold them again. I was so scared shitless that I didn't even think I was holding anything."

He goes on to say:

"The food here sucks, we have a total of about one minute to eat our food. They don't give you silverware, you have to eat with your hands and make sandwiches out of whatever you're eating because everything is time consuming.

Now that I am here at basic I really think about being home. Writing this letter already gave me tears in my eyes. I guess it is because I did not receive any of my mail yet and feel lonely. The more I sit around at night on my free time, I wonder if the army is really for me. You know and I know I can't be gone a long time without getting homesick. It is three weeks today that I've been gone and I'm homesick now. I tried getting airborne school in my contract, but the drill sergeant took Monday off for Columbus day and I shipped out Tuesday. I asked the captain when I got here and he said that if you don't have it on your contract you will not be able to go, and they don't ask at the end of basic anymore. So I'm bummed out that I can't follow in your footsteps. I've been sick and can't breathe out of my nose, and can't stop coughing. Last night I had to get up at 1:00 am for guard duty and had the biggest headache ever from coughing so much. They gave me Ibuprofen 800mg. and something else that is supposed to open my nose. The drill sergeant said that if you go on sick call and miss seventy two hours of basic, you will not graduate and be put in a different class. So maybe I can get myself better without going on sick call. We were told today by the captain that we will graduate on February 17th from basic training and AIT.

He also told us we will be home for Christmas, no matter what.

Well, I'm gonna go now, hope to hear from you soon because I didn't get your first letter yet. Tell Sheila that I said "hello, and I love her." Dad, I love you very, very much and can't wait to see you again. Love you , A.J. XXOO

p.s. - Tell gram and pap I love them.

16 October, 1999. I figured I would write to you again since I have a lot of free time right now. I'm doing alot better now, I'm not really homesick anymore. I'm going to church sometime today so that should help me a lot.

My job will be 11-M which means I will be driving a Bradley or firing the gun.

Is that pretty cool or what? I hear it is a really neat piece of equipment. The Lt. Colonel said I will probably be deployed to Kosovo or Bosnia.

I had to stop writing because of lights out last night, so I figured I would write about today. Well, this morning my company got up at 5:30 to do barracks maintenance. Then at 7:00, we went to breakfast and came back. Some people in my platoon were assholes and we had to do pushups and other physical conditioning.

After that, we went to church and the chaplain asked who would like to join the choir. I stood up and joined the choir. It is kinda funny that when I was growing up the only time I went to church was with you or gram and pap. Just sitting there and listening to the chaplain talk about God made me really happy. I didn't think anything would make me happy than to be at home, but when I went to church it changed my feelings somehow, I don't know how, but it did. The army is really for me, it already has me going to mass and making me a bigger man than what I was when I left home. Would you send me a small bible? It is so weird here, everybody is from hundreds of miles away from each other and never met, but we all feel the same way.

There are too many chiefs in my platoon and it's making a lot of us mad, especially me, because of my short fuse. I'm afraid that I'm going to snap on one of them and I'm going to hurt someone. This one guy I met in my platoon is a really cool guy. He is twenty eight years old and we're getting along great. He's been keeping me away from the idiots, but other than that, I'm doing better.

Love ya, A.J. XOOXOO

20 October, 1999. I figured that I would drop you a line or two since I have some time. The days are starting to go by pretty fast now. We started our PT on Monday morning, and it is a piece of cake. Yesterday we received our M16A1 rifles and started to clean them and get familiar with them. You have to see some of the idiots who have no clue about a gun. One guy said to me,"what is a cleaning kit for?" I could have smacked him, and then he wanted to know what a safety was. I told him not to ask me and to just listen to the drill sergeant. I guess I can't really blame him for not knowing, but he could use some common sense. Then I remembered what you told me about helping guys like that because I might end up sharing a foxhole with one.

Do you remember when you had me over for dinner before I left and we watched "Full Metal Jacket?" The one drill sergeant here looks just like the guy in the movie, I mean, to a tee. By the way, I want two things from you for Christmas. The first is a book called, Blackhawk Down. The reason for the book is that my drill sergeant is in the book and he says that whoever gets it he will sign it for them. Is that cool or what? The other thing is a case of good German beer so I can get used to drinking it before I get stationed somewhere in Europe.

Did Rich shoot a deer? Oh, I forgot, YOU can't shoot a deer if you're golfing all the time. Tell Rich I said hello and also Verna. Make sure you give

Uncle Guy, JoAnn, and Jean Marie my new address or I'll be waiting forever for my mail to come. The weather here is still warm, we wake up every morning to do our PT in our shorts and tee shirts yet. Well, I gotta get going, we have a formation for chow soon. Tell everyone I said hello. Tell gram and pap I love them and please send me stamps. Tell Sheila I'm doing fine and love her also.

Love you, A.J. XOOXOO

2 November, 1999. Well, it is Tuesday, Nov. 2nd, I hope you and Sheila, gram and pap had a good time at Uncle Guy's and that you had a safe trip home. I called on Sunday but you and Uncle Guy had already left to go golfing. Did you beat Uncle Guy or is he better than you and kicked your butt? Tonight I just got my first pay stub, I make $946.88 and bring home $713.41 a month. That's pretty good pay for having fun. The days are going by pretty fast now because we are finally training. Today we went into the, YES, you guessed it, the gas chamber. It was not as bad as I thought it would be. My drill sergeant made me and a couple other guys take off our masks and run around inside singing the Star Spangled Banner, then do five push ups, get up, run in place and recite our name, rank, and serial number. Then we had to say our drill sergeant is number one and our platoon is number one. I thought I was gonna die. I could not see and I had snot hanging down to my knees.

Before we went in we were watching the other platoons coming out and could not stop laughing at them. Boy, I learned my lesson on making fun of people because I got a taste of the same stuff.

The army is a very interesting thing. We went over everything you taught me about life. Don't drink and drive, don't use drugs, have respect for people and things. I'm relearning everything you taught me already, but when I sit in class, I wonder if everything you taught me; did you learn it from the army? Well, besides shooting a gun, because I know you don't know how to shoot one, just like a bow, but when I come home I'll teach you. Thank you for sending stamps and getting that bible for me. Well, I got to go, I must sleep. I have C.Q. duty tonight from 2:00-3:00am, and I have PT at 4:00. I'll write later.

Love ya, A.J. XXOXXO

6 November, 1999. Well, I figured I'd write to you since we have a few hours to ourselves before chow, and because we run eight miles today. Our drill sergeants are preparing us for our twenty five mile road march. Well, I finished my second week today and have twelve more weeks until graduation. I can't wait, we're all pumped up for the big day. We did rappelling on Thursday and it was the "cat's nuts." I had a lot of fun. This week we start basic rifle marksmanship and I hope I

qualify as an expert. They say that if you already know how to shoot, it is harder to qualify because you have your own shooting habits. I like the picture you sent me and my drill sergeant got a kick out of some of the funnies. My drill sergeant is a real down to earth guy. My platoon was getting ready to go on our eight mile run this morning, we were in formation by the side of the road and a nice truck was going by and myself and another soldier looked in the bed of the truck and noticed two tree stands. We looked at one another and said, "Wish it was us." This is a kid I was having problems with since I got here and now we're like best friends, we haven't stopped talking about archery since early this morning.

He was telling me that he is from Missouri and his buddy holds the second biggest Pope & Young record. He says he'll have him send some pictures.

It is pretty neat meeting guys from all around the states who hunt. Tell Rich and Uncle Jim I said "hi." Thanks for the Tums; you can send them anytime because I have heartburn all the time. Well, gotta go. Love you, A.J.

11 November, 1999. Boy, what a great day today, I have not done a thing hard yet. Today is Veteran's Day so we have a four day weekend. Today, we ended Phase One, we had a barracks check; beds, locker, latrine, you know how the inspection thing

works. Yesterday we went to the twenty five meter range to work on sight firing position, aiming point center of mass, breathing control, and trigger squeeze. Then we practiced the dime test where you put a dime on the barrel and you go through all the steps I just mentioned. If the dime falls off you need more practice and if it doesn't fall off, you're an expert, like ME. Then we went into a building that was like a game room. They had the M16A1 as a game and we practiced all those steps again but it was on a video screen, like the type they had out at Heisler's. You had to shoot seven out of nine in a 1cm circle to qualify, and yes, I did it. I got seven out of nine. Man, am I good or what? Good thing I took lessons from the best.

Monday we are marching out to a range that is ten miles away. We're marching with everything we have and then some. We're staying out overnight and that is going to be cool. All week we will be training on different courses, like the stationary and the moving targets. Then the next Monday we qualify and I am going to try to fire expert. Then after that we have hand grenade training and two PT tests. Then we graduate basic and start AIT, after our Christmas leave. Find out for me what you need to do to get assigned to the unit that guards the Tomb of the Unknowns in Washington, D.C. I would like to do that if I don't get airborne school. Oh, tomorrow we are going to play all kinds of sports and then go to the Infantry

Museum. Also, I might be getting my wisdom teeth taken out, my mouth keeps bleeding and I constantly have a sore throat. The stuff you think of when you get ready to stop writing. Okay, I'm signing off for the night.

Love ya, your soldier, Pvt. Baddick, EXPERT SHOOTER, A.J. XOOX

14 November, 1999. Just wanted to write to tell you I got my Halloween card from Uncle Guy. Did you go golfing lately? Maybe if the weather is nice when I come home , and if there are any courses open yet, we could go out again. When I come home, don't tell gram and pap I will be at your house for Christmas, I want to surprise them. I want them to see me in my Class A's.

Yesterday we had sports day and it was fun. We had tug of war, football, baseball, and relay races. My platoon came in second overall.

I forgot to tell you that we had a big inspection the other day with the Lieutenant and First Sergeant. During the inspection my drill sergeant called me to my locker, I got nervous because I knew I had everything squared away. Well, when I got to my locker he pointed to the picture of Harry and he said he had a dog just like him. He asked me who the guy was in the picture in BDU's and jump equipment with the 82nd patch on his shoulder. I told him it was my father and he asked if this was why I joined the military and I told him yes, that I wanted to follow in your footsteps. Then he asked me if that was why I'm such a pain in the ass about going airborne. I told him yes, so he he's going to see if he can help me. That's pretty nice of him. If you run into Laura Banta, give her my address to give to her sister Tracey so Tracey can give it to her boyfriend Dave Stidle so he can write to me. He is the guy I told you about that flies helicopters, Cobras or Apaches. Well, I'm gonna go, see you in a few weeks.

Love you, Soldier Boy A.J. XOXO

19 November, 1999. Well, right now it is about 0400 hrs. and we have a little time this morning so I thought I would start your letter. Sit back in your "Lazy Boy" and enjoy. All the fun started Tuesday at 3:00. The night before we packed our rucksacks with everything we have. The whole company started out to the field at around 0345 hrs. and our destination was a range called Malon 9, which is about seven miles out. We arrived there and we zeroed and grouped our weapons. That took all day until around 1900 hrs. Then we moved out again and road marched two and a half miles to our bivouac site.

This is where all the fun started for me. We were told to set up camp for the night. We used our half man tents and rolled them on the ground, put our sleeping bags on top, and a poncho on top of us and the sleeping bag. Well, gotta go for another day out in the field. I'll finish when I get back. 0415 hrs.

Okay, sit back down again, I'm back. It is 2000 hrs. and bivouacking again. At about 2100 hrs., when we finally got to lie down, the drill sergeants yelled out for mail call, so we got mail out in the field. After that we picked our fire guards and went to sleep, but then we heard live fire, claymores going off, and hand grenades. That is the live fire training that we will be doing when we come back from Christmas leave. It sounded so cool in the middle of the night. After that we heard helicopters flying over, and then they were hovering out in front of us for awhile. The drill sergeant said it was and upcoming ranger class going through some training. After it all got quiet around 0100 hrs. I had fire watch and I heard dogs barking in the distance.

About twenty minutes later they were right at our bivouac area and the drill sergeants fired shots at them to chase them away. They turned out to be a pack of coyotes. Pretty cool, huh?

The MRE's are good but they could add more food to them. Today, we shot at moving targets from 175 to 300 meters. I'm shooting like shit, I don't know what's going on, maybe I'm nervous about qualifying, because if you don't qualify, you get recycled and graduate later.

The weather is great down here, the mornings are getting colder but late in the day, when it gets dark it's great. Sorry about the writing, I haven't gotten much sleep this week. Oh, I almost forgot to tell you. We were at a rifle range yesterday and we were right by the airborne school. When you looked across the road you could see the towers where they were taking the students up in the air with a closed canopy, and when they would drop them straight down, the canopy would open. That was really cool. Well, I gotta go now. I heard we are going to the obstacle course tomorrow. Boy, I wish I had time to take a shit, maybe on Christmas leave.

Happy Thanksgiving. Love, A.J. XOXO

25 November, 1999. Well, it's Thanksgiving Day and my company just got back to the barracks at 0630 hrs. We have been gone since Monday morning. We went to the rifle range to practice our fundamentals Monday, and bivouacked Monday night. Tuesday morning it was PT, like always, and then it was time for qualifying. I was the first to shoot in our platoon. No, I did not get expert because my weapon jammed two times on me. We had to shoot twenty three out of forty to qualify. I shot a twenty nine and missed sharpshooter by one. I ended up getting marksman, but the good

news is that I move on with my class, "Thank God." My company was the first company out of all the infantry recruits who ever came through Ft. Benning for basic, to shoot a 100%. That means that every soldier in my company qualified. We also had the highest number of expert shooters at Ft. Benning beating the old record by one. The old record was twenty six, we had twenty seven. Then Tuesday night we marched 4.5 miles to our next bivouac site. Wednesday we did NBC shooting with our gas masks on and that was hard because the mask gets in the way and you have to cant your weapon to the side to aim.

After that we marched 2 miles to another range that was the best yet because we shot at night with tracers and that is neat to see in person. We shot just about all night long, they must have had alot of ammo to get rid of.

We had four fires that we had to put out on the range because the grass is very dry right now. After we finished, we marched 8.25 miles back to the barracks. I'm having a lot of fun now and we get paid to have fun, I can't believe this government.

Can you get me a book called, Meeting God Behind Enemy Lines by Steve Watkins? He is a Navy Seal who believes God helped him through all his training as a recruit to a seal and beyond that. One of the guys in my platoon has it. Actually, I've been reading it since Friday and it is very good.

Oh, I forgot to tell you that next week we have grenade qualification and live night fire qualification. Then we will be taking it easy from what I hear. Tell Sheila I said "hi" and "Happy Thanksgiving." Also, tell gram and pap I got their card and give them a hug and kiss and thank you from me. Well, I'm gonna go now, I have to go to church in an hour and I still have not slept.

Boy, I feel like I'm going through Ranger School, who knows, maybe I will.

Gotta go, see you in three weeks. Love ya, Private Baddick, Rock Steady.

2 December, 1999. I just spoke to you the other day but wanted to tell you about the weekend. Well, after we all came back from pass we ended up having our bags checked to make sure there was no candy, cigarettes, booze, etc. Yesterday, well, I mean last night after lights out the drill sergeants came into our barracks around 2200 hrs. and tore everything apart. They flipped our bunks upside down, tore everything out of our wall lockers, rucksacks, and even unrolled our sleeping bags. They said it was what they called a Health & Welfare Inspection. I thought it was kinda funny to see them rip everything apart and not find any

contraband. Then we had to have the barracks spotless by 0230 hrs. for an inspection before our road march at 0400 hrs. It was a ten miler and when we got there they drove me back to go to the dentist. I had my upper left and lower left wisdom teeth pulled so now I'm on bed rest and can write my father. Tomorrow we are going for our Class A's. I can't wait until I get them. Only nineteen days left until I come home. I can't wait for the day to come so I can go out hunting.

I think this Army stuff is pretty cool, you go and get your teeth pulled for free, or even go to the doctor for free. In civilian life, you can't do that nowhere I can think of.

How was your Thanksgiving? Mine was okay, I wish I were home and eating turkey. They ran out of turkey here, can you believe it? They can't even feed an Army Boy. I'm gonna go, I'll see you for Christmas.

Love ya, A.J. Rock Steady

4 December, 1999. I got your card the other day and I have it hanging on my locker door to remind me to give it all I got everyday and to kick ass.

Next Saturday I will be in a marathon run for children who have parents that can't afford to buy them presents. The army picks five of the fastest runners from each company to run. I was the second fastest in our company with a two mile run of 13:13."

Today, we're doing the bayonet course. Oh, the drill sergeant made me platoon guide because he says I have alot of discipline, respect, and I'm highly motivated. I hope I can keep control of fifty five animals.

I don't have a Christmas list because I don't really need anything while I'm here. Two weeks till I come home. I can't wait to see you, Sheila, and Harry.

I had to stop writing for awhile, we had to get ready for the bayonet course.

That was a lot of fun but man, I thought I was gonna die before I even finished the course. I just kept going and pushing myself to do the 110% that is expected of me. You should have seen how dirty and muddy I was, my whole body was covered in it. Next week is our 8th week and also it is my last week of basic, then when I come back we start AIT. I guess we're going to be learning about the AT4. It is used to blow up tanks. We're also going to be throwing hand grenades and learning about claymore mines.

Oh, and also we'll be doing pugil stick fighting and hand to hand. So I hope the next two weeks go by fast. Well, I'm gonna get going, see you soon.

Love you, A.J. Rock Steady.

p.s. - Why is the sky blue? Because God loves infantrymen."

A.J. came home for the Christmas of 1999 and what a wonderful Christmas it was. He had asked us not to tell his gram and pap he was coming home so he could surprise them. Oh boy, were they surprised, they both had tears in their eyes. His sister, Elizabeth, couldn't believe it. She told me, "dad, that's not my brother, they sent the wrong A.J. home. He's so polite, everything is "yes ma'am" and "no ma'am. And he looks so good." Of course, I thought he looked great. When he went away to basic A.J. was just a tall string bean. Now my son had filled out some, in the upper torso area, he was looking buff. He had on his new class A uniform and he looked like a real soldier. We had Christmas that year at our house for the family. In attendance were Elizabeth and her husband Terald Hoherchak (we call him Shack), Sheila's daughter Tyna, her husband Rick Dierolf, and their daughter Kaitlyn, my Mom and Dad, and Sheila's Mom and Dad (Donald & Gloria). There was also my Aunt Eleanor Paslawsky, and her two daughters Joann (who is Andrew's Godmother), and Jean Marie. My cousin Jim Bialek, and his wife Beth came, with her niece, Becca. We had a great time, everyone was so happy to see A.J. and he was obviously glad to be home. Kaitlyn was parading around with A.J.'s uniform hat on. There were quite a few pictures taken and you could see A.J. was growing tired of posing after about the first dozen or so. I said, "son, I'm thinking that maybe you'd like to get out of your uniform and put on your jeans and sweatshirt and relax a bit." He looked at me and was in total agreement. After we opened presents and filled our bellies with delicious food and things died down a bit, I noticed my son over in my recliner, stretched out, sleeping, with Harry by his side. He looked very content.

I told A.J. his Aunt Genevieve, my Dad's sister, wanted to see him. She mostly stayed in her house because it was on the second floor and she had a very hard time negotiating the one hundred steps up to it. We took a trip to Mexico a few years a back and visited the ancient Mayan city of Chichen Itza. They had a temple there that we climbed and that's what Aunt Gen's stairway reminds me of. Anyway, A.J. and I dropped by to see Aunt Gen and she was thrilled to see him. There was a package delivered to her outside door so she told (she didn't ask, ever), A.J. to bring it in and told me to open it. Then she had a poinsettia plant in the kitchen that someone gave her. She told A.J. to take it into her spare bedroom. Then she told A.J. to go get her purse, she wanted to give him some money for Christmas. Then she told A.J. to go down the steps and get her mail, which he promptly did for her. Aunt Gen was a hard task master but she was always good to me and my brother. We finally said goodbye and when we got in the car A.J. turned to me and said, "Wow dad, Aunt Gen could be one of my drill sergeants." I should have sent him over to live with her for a few weeks before basic.

Well, his Christmas vacation came to an end and A.J. headed back to Ft. Benning to complete his training. He finished his AIT training with Echo Co. 1/19th Infantry. I still have and use a coffee mug A.J. sent home to me with the 19th Infantry insignia on it. He found out he would be going to Ft. Hood, Texas for his first assignment with the 4th Infantry Division (Mechanized), The Ivy Division.

WHITE LIGHTNING

Chapter 5

A.J. called home when he arrived at Ft. Hood. He said it was nice there and he was proud to be able to sew the 4th Infantry Division patch on his shoulder. He did some research and found out that the 4th Inf. Div. had a real history, and he thought this would be a good stop for him. It was a good stop for my son. As time went by A.J. made some good friends there. He met a guy whose family owned a big ranch in Texas and A.J. said he was invited to go there when they got leave to do some hunting. A.J. asked me if I would send him his bow and I complied with his request. Life was becoming somewhat normal for him, he had new friends, hunting was again an option for him, and he enjoyed his new home in the military. He sent me pictures once of a trip he and his friends made to Galveston. It must have been a wild time for A.J., the pictures were taken on the beach and he said you could drive your personal vehicles on it. He had photos, of mostly big, 4-wheel trucks, people crammed in the back partying, some barbecuing, and one photo of girls going by in the back of a truck showing off their headlights (if you know what I mean).

They were doing some training out in the field and they were supposed to attack a position. A.J. told me one guy with an M-60 machinegun was advancing to slow so he grabbed the M-60 off of the guy and raced forward helping to overrun the position. He said one of the guys gave him the nickname of "White Lightning" because he was so fast. He loved it, thought it was great.

A.J. seemed to be doing really well at Ft. Hood. He was offered a new job as a Bradley Fighting Vehicle driver. He said it was the best thing yet, it was like driving a 4-wheeler through the woods. He said you could go anywhere with it, there was no stopping it. He said going to the firing range was a hoot because firing the main gun, a 25mm cannon was so neat. A.J. said he would like to go deer hunting with it. Things went well for A.J. in Texas and he was soon promoted to Specialist. He was very proud of himself.

He called home one day and told me he was informed his enlistment was coming to an end and that he would have to get out of the army or re-enlist. I said, "I thought you enlisted for four years" and he said he thought he did too. There must have been some kind of mistake made. Anyway, he called me a few days later informing me that he told them he would re-enlist for six years if they would send him to jump school and then to the 82nd Airborne Division. They honored his request, gave him a nice bonus, and sent him to jump school a few months later.

Before he left for Ft. Benning, his unit had to go on special assignment to some base in Arkansas to pull guard duty at a chemical munitions storage facility. He said when they arrived it was pouring down rain and they had nowhere to put them up for the night so they pulled out their ponchos and made two man tents for the night. A.J. said it was damp and cold but he sucked it up because that was his job and he was glad to do it. He was on his way to take a nice hot shower the next day and had to pass through a wooded area. A.J. kicked up the biggest buck he had ever seen, saying its rack came out past its ears at least five inches on each side, and looked to be about an eight or ten pointer. Seems my son just can't get away from those deer.

Well, the Christmas season of 2001 was approaching and my son called me on the phone to give me some news, and some news it was. He had decided that he was going to get married for New Years. I will admit that I didn't take the news too well, since A.J.'s life was going fairly well at this time and I didn't feel that his getting married would help at this particular time. However, I remember telling my father the same thing while I was in the army and his reply was, "good for you son." So I decided I would just have to accept my son's decision, but I was still not particularly thrilled with the idea. His new wife's name was Jamie, and she was from Pittsburgh, Pennsylvania. A home girl, so how bad could it be?

While A.J. was stationed at Ft. Hood he became friends with Sgt. Patrick Sowers. Patrick's father was in the military and as an Army brat, he grew up at Ft. Hood, Texas. Patrick spent eight years serving our country, and when he met A.J. he was with Bravo Company, 2-8 Infantry, 4th Inf. Div. They were in the same platoon together and Patrick was A.J.'s Team Leader. Patrick said, "I knew him well. I knew he had an airborne tattoo even though he had not even gone to airborne school yet. I was a sniper team leader in 2001 and A.J. expressed a lot of interest in learning this trait, but his main passion was always about going airborne. We went out and drank together, and he was always the one guy that you could depend on to be there, except when it came to being the designated driver. He was always laughing and always talking about home; always talking about home. When I learned A.J. died, I actually cried. It's hard for a soldier and a man to admit that, but as an NCO you always take responsibility, even though you are not there, because you feel you should have been. The one thing I remember about A.J. was that he was a soldier, a soldier's soldier, always there for anyone that needed help. Funny, that should have been his middle name, soldier. A.J. liked to drink, and when he drank he was always laughing and making jokes. I still think the airborne tattoo was probably the funniest thing, he always wanted to go to airborne school, so everyone thought it was funny that he had the tattoo before he even went."

Patrick now runs a store in Dallas, Texas, to assist our troops returning from overseas. He is the founder of a non-profit organization that provides financial assistance and support to returning soldiers. Through donations, they have assisted military families with furniture, computers, cosmetics and hygiene products, food, and other necessary items to make their lives easier. The website is www.operationonceinalifetime.com.

Patrick Sowers has a memorial to Sgt. A.J. Baddick in his store, which consists of the military boots, rifle, and helmet. Thank you for your service to our country Patrick, and for your continuing work with our returning heroes.

So, weeks passed and my son was back at Ft. Benning where he started. It was January of 2002. Now he was over at the jump towers that he gazed at before with such jealousy. Wow, was he ever excited. You could just hear it in his voice when he called home. "I'm here, I'm finally here, dad." Having been through jump school I knew what he was in for. No matter where you go, you go at the double time, which means running. It sure keeps you in shape.

A week of jumping off platforms to practice your PLF's, parachute landing falls. They teach you how to hit the ground without breaking your ankles or legs. Then a week of learning how to exit the airplane properly. Stand in the door, hop out into oblivion, and count, one one thousand, two one thousand, three one thousand, four one thousand. Look up to see if you have a full parachute canopy above your head. In practice you jump out of an airplane mockup about fifty feet in the air. Your harness is attached to a cable and after you stop falling, you slide along the cable to a collection area where two guys stop you and unhook your harness. Then they have to run back toward the tower with your harness so another trainee can get hooked up.

The third week is tower week. Now A.J. was going to become well acquainted with those huge two hundred and fifty foot towers he used to be so envious of. The towers have four arms protruding from the top. Each arm has a frame to connect an open parachute to it. Only three arms are used at a time because of the wind, you can't have a trainee coming down headed right at the tower. That wouldn't do. So, the frames are lowered, a chute is connected to them and a trainee is harnessed to each chute. Trainees are then raised to the top of the towers. The view from up there is incredible.

Down below, the instructors, called black hats (because they wear black baseball hats), are on bullhorns giving last minute instructions. Once they are finished, the black hats ask for a thumbs-up from the trainees. If they get a thumbs up, the trainees are released totally on their own. They learn to steer their chutes away from the tower and hopefully, remember how to land without breaking something.

Then comes that final week when you do your required five jumps from an airplane. That is the best part of jump school. I remember one class we had dealing with landing in trees. The black hats told us that if we were ever caught in trees, we were to undo our harnesses and get to the ground in the safest manner possible. We were told never to try to extricate our chutes from the trees because they cost a lot of money and the government didn't want them ripped needlessly. On one of my jumps at Ft. Benning, someone in the plane hesitated causing those of us in the back of the plane to jump late. After my chute opened I noticed that I was over a blacktop road and so I grabbed one side of my harness to steer my chute away. I sure didn't want to land on any surface as hard as a road. I made it over the road but landed in some trees and ended up down a small embankment. A short time later I heard the sound of a vehicle stopping and looked up to see some black hats. They asked first if I was alright and I told them I was. Next, they asked me if I could grab onto the apex of my chute (the center), and hand it up to them. I did as instructed and the next thing they did was hook it onto the back of the jeep and drive away ripping it to shreds. So much for being careful with government property.

While A.J. was going through jump school, my father passed away. We called A.J. to tell him the bad news. My mom was staying with us and she got on the phone with her grandson; he was crying, and said he was coming home for pap's funeral. My mom told him to stay where he was and complete jump school, that his pap would have wanted it that way. She told him his pap was in heaven looking down on him, smiling, and very proud of him. "You stay right there and get your jump wings honey, pap understands, he's with you always" my mother said.

Anyway, A.J. made it through jump school and got his wings. He was now parachute qualified and stood a little taller in his boots. He was proud he was no longer a leg, a term used for all those other people in the military who are not jump qualified. Next stop: Ft. Bragg, North Carolina, home of the 82nd Airborne Division, America's Guard of Honor.

ALL AMERICAN

Chapter 6

A.J. arrived at Ft. Bragg, N.C. sometime in March, 2002. He was assigned to Headquarters & Headquarters Company, and was given a job as driver for a Major at the Assault Command Post. He called and let me know that he was finally an All American. The 82nd patch has AA on it. When the original unit was formed during the First World War, there happened to be one man from each state, so it was called the All American Unit. Sgt. Alvin York, who received the Medal of Honor in World War I was a member of the 82nd Division. It was not yet an airborne unit, but became airborne during World War II. Following the surrender of Germany, the 82nd was ordered to Berlin for occupation duty. In Berlin, General George Patton was so impressed with the 82nd's honor guard, he said, "In all my years in the Army, and all the honor guards I have ever seen, the 82nd's honor guard is undoubtedly the best." Hence, the "All Americans" became known as "America's Guard of Honor."

A.J.'s wife Jamie had found them housing off-post and my son seemed to be quite content with his life. They came home for a visit and it gave A.J.'s new wife a chance to meet the family. Everyone decided to chip in and give the new married couple some home furnishings to take back with them. They had some furniture, tables, wall hangings, a bed, lamps, and many other assorted items. We also decided to give A.J. his pap's car. On the day they left to go back to Ft. Bragg, we rented them a U-Haul truck and a car carrier on the back for the car. They made it back safe and sound and set up house.

As soon as the weather warmed up Sheila and I decided to take a trip to Ft. Bragg and visit the newlyweds. My mother also accompanied us and she really enjoyed the trip. It was May of 2002. Now, I had been stationed at Ft. Bragg back in the early '70s but I was in for quite a shock. I hardly recognized the base, it had become so large over the years that I had to ask directions when we got there. Interestingly enough, when I had six months left to serve, Sheila and her first husband were just arriving at Ft. Bragg. Of course, we never knew one another, but what a coincidence to find that out years later when we met.

I asked A.J. where his pap's car was and he told me he sold it. I asked why and he said it needed new tires and work on the engine and he didn't have the money for that, and they could use the money from the sale. I told him his pap would be happy that he was able to help him out with some extra money.

We decided we would have a cookout, but there was no grill to cook on, so Sheila and I took A.J. to the local Wal-Mart and we bought them a nice grill, already assembled so we could use it right away. After we dropped off Sheila and the grill, my son and I headed for the PX center so we could get some beverages. I told A.J. to grab whatever he wanted to drink, so he pulled two cases of Yeungling Lager from the cooler. I said to him, "Nothing like drinking the old home favorite, I didn't know you could get it here." He looked at me with a smile and replied, "Oh yeah."

We headed back to his place and as we were unloading the beer from the car he pointed out a guy to me and said, "He just moved in a few doors down, he's a captain and he's from Pennsylvania." I told A.J. to grab a few cans of beer and follow me. We went over to the new guy's door and I knocked. He opened the door and I introduced myself and my son and said, "My son tells me you're from Pennsylvania, here's a house warming gift for you." He laughed and we told him we were having a cookout and he was invited. He told us he had some paperwork to take care of on post but said he'd try to stop by later. As we walked away I told A.J. that it never hurts to make new friends, especially those with captain's bars.

The cookout was a blast. Some of the neighbors were there and they were all military types. There were burgers, hot dogs, and one of the guys made his special barbequed ribs and they were excellent. One of the guys was Special Forces and A.J. had a very good relationship with him. A.J. seemed to think that was the direction his career would take him in. My mom really enjoyed herself and truly liked the company. There's just something about military people that makes you feel at home. We brought along an inflatable air mattress to sleep on and it was quite comfortable. However, the next morning when Sheila and I awoke, we were surprised to find that all the air had leaked out of the mattress. We were lying on the floor and I had my share of aches and pains.

Later in the day we went to the pool for a swim. My mom went along and relaxed in a pool chair. My mother was legally blind at the time. She had macular degeneration, which meant that when she looked at an object it was blurred but all around it was fairly clear. As we sat there by the pool, A.J. started to do some horse playing with Jamie and as she ran by us my mom looked over at me and said, "wow, Jamie sure has a big set of water wings on her." Now, I find it interesting that my mom would notice that, or should I say them? I guess Jamie's hooters were rather large if my mother noticed them.

We went for a ride later on and we asked A.J. if he could find the place where I lived when I was at Ft. Bragg. He did indeed find the place but it was fairly run down. It was a trailer park but we had some great times when we lived there. Elizabeth was born at Ft. Bragg; yep, she was an army brat.

One of my best friends in the army was a guy named Tony Ravenda, who hailed from East Rutherford, New Jersey. He was married and had a little girl. They would spend a lot of time at our trailer with us. After we got out of the army, Tony drove the family to Pennsylvania for a visit. We had a great time, but the thing I remember most was that it was wintertime, and as we prepared to say goodbye, the car tires kept spinning and their car couldn't get up a slight grade behind our house. I told Tony to put it in park and I went down into the cellar for a tub of ashes. I brought them up to his car and sprinkled them underneath his tires. Then I told him, "pull out slow and steady." After they made it up the grade and stopped the car, Tony leaned out the window and said, "They worked great, where'd you get them?" I replied, "I have a machine in the basement that makes them." Me and Tony had some good times together.

On another visit, we were driving out of Jim Thorpe, on Broadway, and Tony said, "stop the car." I asked what was wrong and he just kept saying, "stop the car." So I did, and we all got out and Tony was saying, "this is beautiful." I asked him what he meant and he said, "the stream flowing by right here, it's just beautiful." I replied, "man, if you think this is beautiful, wait until we get to Tuscarora State Park." When we arrived at Tuscarora, we took Tony's family on a walk around the park and he just couldn't get over the fact that it was all free. Later on, we drove into Tamaqua so they could see my mom and dad, since they had met previously at Ft. Bragg. The subject of fire companies came up, and my dad was explaining to Tony how we had four volunteer fire companies in town. He was totally amazed that a small town like Tamaqua could have that many fire companies, and all of them volunteer. Tony said that was quite an accomplishment and something to be proud of. I guess living in that area most of our lives, we took those things we showed Tony's family, for granted. Sometimes we just don't realize how lucky we are.

Sheila wanted to look for the shopping center where she used to work. It was called Bordeaux, and out front there was a small Eiffel Tower. Sheila used to work in a shoe store there. We drove around for quite awhile but A.J. finally found it.

I had mentioned to A.J. that before we left I wanted to go buy an airborne license plate for the front of my car. He reached behind the chair and pulled one out and gave it to me. He said it was a present for me. I still have it on the front of my car to this day. It's black with silver jump wings.

Well, the next day we said our goodbyes and headed home. It was hard to leave but we got through it, though not without a tear in my eye.

THE SANDBOX

Chapter 7

A.J. deployed to Afghanistan in August of 2002 with Headquarters Company, 82nd Airborne Division. On the flight there they had some engine trouble and had to divert to Incurlik, Turkey. They were there for about three days until they could make repairs. They flew in a C-17 and A.J. was invited to sit in the cockpit during the flight and was able to observe the plane being refueled in flight. They finally arrived at Bahgram airbase and A.J. said it was the hottest and dirtiest place he had ever been. When he got there the weather was in the one hundreds. He said that they received small arms fire a lot of the time and it was kind of scary. For the first two weeks he lived in a twenty man tent called a GP Medium. August began a period called the "120 days of wind." "It was a constant hot, dry wind. Never less than twenty miles per hour and as high as eighty miles per hour. The wind picked up our tents and blew them over." On top of the one hundred twenty dry degrees every day, the local waters were polluted and bottled water had to be flown in from

Germany. "I didn't get a shower for close to five weeks, until showers were built. Until then we took showers using bottled water." By January, the weather turned cold and wet, with temperatures of twenty degrees. "It only snowed once, on Christmas eve. We went out and threw snowballs at one another." A.J. met local Afghan men hired by the army to build housing and shower areas. "They helped us and we helped to stimulate their economy. We worked and spoke with the Afghans everyday. They were happy we were there to help them and make their lives better. [My unit] told me they needed an RTO so I accepted the job. They gave me two minutes of training and I had to learn the rest by myself."

As an RTO, A.J. monitored the incoming air waves and transmitted the information to aircraft and ground forces. He quickly learned the call signs and the way the pilots needed the information. "I had to understand the difference between an air grid and a ground grid. Trying to transform one to the other was the hardest.

One day, A.J. was walking with five officers when suddenly they began taking rocket and small arms fire. Two rockets landed one hundred yards from them. They took cover as they were pelted by small arms fire. "We tried to return fire but were unable to find out where it was coming from. It lasted no more than five minutes. We stayed under cover as best we could and then snuck away." Though that was A.J.'s closest call he said he had buddies that were shot at just about every day.

While A.J. was in Afghanistan, I decided to erect a flagpole outside our house. It was a labor of love in my son's honor. When it was all ready to go, I invited our neighbors over for the flag raising. I raised the flag of the United States of America and directly under it was the flag of the 82nd Airborne Division. Both flags still have a place of honor on the flagpole to this day. Of course, they have been replaced numerous times. Our neighbors joined us in pledging allegiance to the flag and then I raised them for the first time. We took pictures and sent them to A.J. over in Afghanistan.

It was around Thanksgiving and the base received a visit from General Tommy Franks. A.J. called home to tell us that the general was up on a platform making a speech to the troops and when he finished he came down the steps and grabbed him in a headlock and proceeded to give him a noogie (rubbing his head furiously with his knuckles) saying, "Baddick, I love your haircut (bald), you're gonna join me and my wife in our tent for Thanksgiving dinner." How could he disobey the orders of a general? He said it was a Thanksgiving he would never forget. He had some nice photos taken with General Franks that we still enjoy looking at. The general also gave my son his challenge coin, and of all the coins I have, his is rather unique because it is in the shape of a dog tag.

A.J. spent six months at Baghram and he said it was rough. The local newspaper did an article on him and he said the worst thing was the loneliness, being away from family and friends and wondering what was going to happen. Just not having a hug, not petting the dog, or not going to McDonalds to grab a burger, but then, that's a huge part of a soldier's life. A.J. came home to Ft. Bragg but it wasn't much of a homecoming. He got off the plane and watched as all the other soldier's families came over to greet them, but there was no one there to meet A.J. He would learn later that his wife had packed up all her belongings and went home to Pittsburg, leaving him with a broken heart. Elizabeth called me and told me what had happened. She said A.J. was lost, had bills that needed to be paid, and he didn't even know how to write a check. After I hung up the phone with my daughter I called A.J. and asked him if he would like me to come down to Ft. Bragg and help him. He told me he would like that, so I immediately left and headed south. I drove almost straight through and on the way I called A.J. and asked him where we could meet and grab a bite to eat. He told me the Cracker Barrel right off of Interstate 95. When I arrived there and met up with my son I wrapped my arms around him and gave him a huge hug and kiss. I asked how he was doing and he said, "not so good." I told him not to worry now that I was there. I said we would get a good meal under our belts and then take on the task at hand.

After eating we headed for the Judge Advocate General's office (JAG), to find out what his legal options were. When we went in, there was a sign stating that the previous day was the day for inquiries and the office we needed was closed. I told A.J. I wasn't leaving until I got to speak with someone. We waited around for about twenty minutes and a female specialist approached and I motioned to her. She asked if she could help us and I explained the situation and said I had just driven from Pennsylvania and really needed to speak with a lawyer. She said she would find out if one was available for us. She returned a short time later and informed us that a captain would be in his office shortly and he would listen to our story if we wanted to wait. I told her I would be on the bench outside his office until he showed up. The captain arrived and ushered us into his office. He told us he couldn't give us much time because he was packing for his deployment to Afghanistan, and as we talked he started to put things into boxes. I explained to him that while my son was serving his country in Afghanistan, his wife took off on him and left him with all the bills. The captain said he understood A.J.'s situation but he was still responsible for what his wife left behind. I thanked the captain for his time and we left. Next stop was the realty office that leased Jamie the house she lived in. It was not the original place they lived before he left for Afghanistan. A nice woman explained to A.J. that his wife signed a lease and he would have to continue paying it, however, she said she would do all she could to find new tenants to take it over as soon as possible. I thanked he for her help and we left for the house. It was a very nice house. I told A.J. to give me all the bills. I called the electric company, the phone company, the garbage company, and one or two others. After telling them what happened they were happy to let A.J. make minimum payments, in fact, he got some money back from the phone company after he closed the account.

Next, we moved anything he wanted out to his truck and my car, to be transported to on post housing, the barracks. Everything else we took out for the garbage and then we cleaned the house. We told the realty lady we would do that for her and she agreed to get it leased.

The following month the house was leased to new people. I spent a few days with my son and it was a good time for the both of us, palling around and enjoying each other's company. I slipped him a few bucks and by the time I left A.J. was sitting pretty. His finances were a bit stretched for a few of his future pays but there was light at the end of the tunnel and he told me he felt much better. Now, finally, he could concentrate on his job and his career, and he did. Knowing that A.J. was relieved and in better spirits made my long drive home more bearable.

A RED DEVIL

Chapter 8

A.J. called one day and said the first sergeant told him he would have to go to one of the line companies. At the time, the 82nd had three line companies, the 325th infantry, the 504th infantry, and the 505th infantry. The first sergeant asked A.J. which one he would like to go to and A.J. said, "the 504th first sergeant." The first sergeant asked him why, and A.J. proudly replied, "because my dad was in the 504th first sergeant." He asked A.J. if he could prove it and A.J. opened his locker and pointed to an old black and white photo of me in my 82nd gear. The first sergeant said it was good enough for him and since he already did six months in Afghanistan, he would make it so A.J. could go to the 504th.

I had the pleasure of speaking to Command Sgt. Major Frank Hacker, who hails from Wilson, Kansas, about my son. He vividly recalled the first time he met A.J. Apparently, my son hadn't told me everything. The reason he was going down to the 504th was because he had pissed someone off at division. When he informed Sgt. Major

Hacker whom he had pissed off, it pleased the Sgt. Major, because he didn't see eye to eye with that individual. He wouldn't divulge the individual's name to me, but said he told A.J. to attend the one week airborne leadership course, and to return after completion of the course, and he would give A.J. a job. A.J. returned on Friday with a shit eatin' grin on his face and a certificate in his hand. Sgt. Major Hacker told him to report to A. Company, that he had found himself a new home.

My son called me that night and was ecstatic, proclaiming, "Dad, guess what, I'm finally a red devil, I'm in first battalion, 504th." He was so proud of himself and I was so happy for him. The 504th Parachute Infantry Battalion is nicknamed "Devils in Baggy Pants." The name was taken from an entry in a German officer's diary in WWII, whose unit opposed the 504th during the Anzio invasion. "American parachutists – 'devils in baggy pants' – are less than 100 meters from my outpost line. I can't sleep at night; they pop up from nowhere and we never know when or how they will strike next. Seems like the black-hearted devils are everywhere..." It was around this time that A.J. was promoted to E-5, Sergeant. He called with the news and said he was now in charge of a squad and he was a bit worried because it was a lot more responsibility. I told him to make sure his guys knew how he wanted them to operate and to take good care of his men. I let him know that he would do well as a squad leader and that I was very proud of him.

Well, A.J. was only in the 504th a short time when he called us to say they were being deployed to Iraq. He said he was coming home for a few days but I wasn't supposed to tell his gram, he wanted to surprise her. He asked me if we could get some flowers for her so we went out and got her a dozen roses. A.J. knocked on her door, and when she opened it, he said, "Flower delivery for Mrs. Baddick." Now remember, my mom was legally blind. She asked, "who would be sending me flowers?" A.J. said, "me gram." She was so excited and happy, she started to cry. My mom held onto her grandson for dear life. It was a beautiful thing to see. My mother was an amazing woman. As long as I can remember, she never complained about anything.

Our home life was simple, and although we had everything we needed, there was never extra money for extravagant things. I never heard my mom say, "I wish we had this, or I wish we could go on a big vacation, or I wish things were better." It's as if she just knew this was the way things were supposed to be, and she made the most of it. Even after my dad passed away, she was still upbeat and kept a positive attitude. My mom was diabetic and had to give herself a shot twice a day. Having Macular Degeneration sure didn't help matters but I would stop in to see her once a week and fill all her needles for her. Still, I never heard a complaint from her. My mom has been a true role model for me, and I have strived to be like her in my own outlook on life. Thanks mom.

We planned a going away cookout at our house for A.J. The family and our neighbors were on hand to bid A.J. a fond farewell. The cookout was great and my son ate like there wouldn't be any food where he was going. I made my famous hot wings and they went fast. Of course, there was plenty of A.J.'s favorite beverage on hand, Yeungling

Lager. Elizabeth took a beautiful picture of me and my son sitting on the back porch, my arm around him. It was our last photo together.

The time came for A.J. to hit the road so everyone said their goodbyes and I walked A.J. out to his car. I told him to do his best and we hugged and kissed for the last time. He said, "dad, if anything happens to me over there, I want to be buried in Arlington." I told him, "okay", shrugging it off, as if anything bad would happen to my son. As he drove away I had tears in my eyes. My son was headed for his second deployment in the global war on terrorism.

THE CANAL

Chapter 9

Sgt. Andrew J. Baddick arrived in Iraq in the fall of 2003, as a member of the Third Brigade Combat Team, A Company, 1/504th Parachute Infantry Regiment, 82nd Airborne Division. He wrote a letter saying it was very hot and that it "sucks worse than Afghanistan, I would go back there any day." Their new base was medieval, having no phones or electric. They rigged up a shower out of two-by-fours and a fifty five gallon drum, "just like on the TV show M.A.S.H." He said it was really hot and asked me to send him a magazine holder for a thirty round mag that straps to your leg and also a fly swatter. Seems like he thought he had a lot of killing to do, the enemy and the flies.

A.J. said one day he was asked to go out with some foreign troops to the firing range and familiarize them with our weapons. He said it was great because he got to fire a lot of Soviet Bloc weapons that they had. When they finished, he said they were standing around talking and A.J. asked them if they were allowed to have booze. He said almost in unison, they all reached inside their jackets and pulled out flasks, telling him, "drink, drink, my friend." A.J. said it was very good and asked them what it was. They said their parents make it and send it to them. I told him it was probably their version of boilo. Where we live, in Northeast Pennsylvania, the locals make something called boilo. It is usually made from grain alcohol, heated on the stovetop, with different spices and fruits added. Great care must be exercised when making it since heating grain alcohol on the stovetop can become dangerous. My cousin, Jim Bialek, was making boilo and wasn't paying attention and he blew out the ceiling tiles over the stove. Everyone has their own secret recipe and some are much better than others.

Iraqi religion frowns on alcohol and the U.S. military strictly adheres to that concept. Once, I sent a package to A.J. and I had purchased those little airline bottles of booze for him. I hid about eight of them in different items inside the package. Later, I received a letter from my son telling me he didn't want to get in trouble for the booze so he gave them to his superior. I told him he was nuts, what did he think his superior did with them? I told him he should have disposed of the evidence at once. He said cigars were like gold over there so I sent him a humidor packed with cigars. A.J. wasn't much of a cigar smoker but he said they were good for trading for what he needed. There's one thing about the army, whatever you need, you can always swap something you have for something someone else has. It's like that old saying: one man's junk is another man's treasure.

I received a letter from A.J. written on September 19, 2003 and in it he explains to me what he was doing there. In the beginning of the week, Bravo Co. was on a convoy and got hit by an IED (improvised explosive device), which killed one of their soldiers. An Iraqi came up to their gate and told the soldier on duty that men were gathering intel on their compound. At the time, his platoon was on quick reaction force duty so they went to the location and searched the buildings and arrested six Iraqis. A.J. said that they had them on the ground, hands tied, with their guns pointed at their heads. He thought that was a bit scary because he said I always taught him to never point a weapon at someone, but then, something clicked in his head and he thought, no more Mr. Niceguy, these sons of bitches could kill me or my guys and he wasn't going to let that happen on his watch.

The next day was calm until dark and then the compound next to them started taking mortar and RPG (rocket propelled grenade) fire. His unit responded but they were too late to nab the bad guys. They were driving back to their compound when they noticed some guys on a rooftop, so they searched that building and took the guys on the roof into custody.

The next evening A.J. was trying to get some sleep when their compound came under mortar and RPG attack. The quick reaction force responded but they found no one. He said they use a lot of hit and run tactics, fire a few rounds and then hightail it to safety. A.J. said he really liked being a sergeant but it was a lot of hard work. He signed off in the letter telling me he was very tired and wore out so he was going to try and get some rest. The last line in the letter said, "remember what we talked about when I was home about my wishes." He was referring to Arlington National Cemetery.

The next and last letter I received from my son was written on September 28, 2003. I thought I would share the letter in its entirety:

"Dear Dad, How are you doing? I'm doing just fine, I guess. The weather over here is really hot still, but the nights are really cool. It's refreshing.

My platoon just got done pulling security for our compound, up in the towers, watching for threats towards us. Yesterday I was put in charge of a fifteen man detail. It was the best detail I was ever put on. We worked with EOD (explosives ordinance detail), out of Ft. Stewart. We loaded up 33,000 lbs. of explosives recovered from the Iraqi's since the start of the war. We loaded everything from hand grenades to rockets that they would put on jets if they had them. Some of them were that big and heavy that we used a crane to load and unload them. We unloaded them in the desert, and I got to play with C-4 (plastic explosive). We used 1,500 pounds of C-4 to blow up the cache. It was a big ass boom and a fireball. Well, tomorrow my platoon is leaving our compound to go and guard a prison here. There are National Guard troops there now, but every night they are getting small arms fire and mortared. So now they are sending in the best, 82nd Airborne baby. Now I will be able to put on my resume that I was guarding a prison in Iraq during the war. I don't know if you have been on the news site or anything reading about us, but we have a reporter from Fayetteville here with us that writes about us. But send me the articles you read on us. I don't know if you know where I am at, but I'm in a really bad spot right now. We are just outside of Baghdad and Fallujah. If you heard of RPG Alley, that is a road we travel often, it is Highway 10. But anyway, I spoke to Nikki yesterday for ten minutes on a satellite phone. She said she was talking to Liz. I am praying for her and I love her, just like I pray for you and Sheila and love you too.

Tell everyone I am fine and doing well. The only time I have been scared is when we travel Highway 10, but I pray to the Blessed Mother to keep me and my men safe. I also pray to pap that he is watching over me and I know that the shadow I see behind me everyday is pap keeping me safe. I know he is so proud of me.

I was reading short stories out of a book from families of soldiers and soldiers themselves that they wrote home. They really touched my heart.

But the one I read was about Leyte and how the men fought there. It was something else. There is a book out that I would like you to send me. I'm not sure who the author is but it is called, "The Hunt for Bin Laden." Also, will you send me baby wipes, lots of them, cause I have only taken two showers my whole time here and I use baby wipes to wipedown. Also, I need a new maglite and a headlamp to read at night. Well dad, I'm gonna go and I love you and miss you. Please write back and let me know how everything is.

Love, A.J."

That was the last thing I ever heard from my son. I'm not sure if the shadow my son was seeing was his pap's or if it was Death coming to take him. I have pondered that in my head for years, and still do. The very next day, A.J. would die.

When the 3rd Brigade Combat Team returned home from Iraq, Sheila and I would receive a visit from A.J.'s Commander, Colonel Jefforey A. Smith, his Company Commander, Captain Rick Belestri, the Company Chaplain, and Sgt. First Class Kulikowski. We greeted them and Captain Belestri said they felt right at home with the 82nd Airborne flag flying outside. I told them my house would always be a safe haven for any member or veteran of the 82nd Airborne Division. We sat around the dining room table, and after offering their condolences, Colonel Smith began to explain, in detail, the events of the evening that A.J. died. It was a very thorough briefing and the following is taken from Colonel Smith's Official Fatality Report, fellow soldiers in A.J.'s unit, and a member of the Kentucky National Guard:

"On the 29th of September, 2003, Alpha Company, 1/504th Parachute Infantry Regiment, was assigned the mission of conducting combat patrols and ambushes in the area immediately surrounding the Abu Ghraib prison, in order to destroy anti-coalition forces responsible for recent mortar attacks. Under the direction of the Alpha Company commander, Captain Rick Balestri, third platoon arrived at the prison and began planning, in conjunction with the commanders of the Kentucky National Guard's 223rd Military Police battalion. A Company was given two main missions: 1) conduct counter-mortar ambushes and patrols to destroy enemy mortar crews and, 2) conduct daytime patrols in the surrounding community to deliver information-operations themes, and make assessments on potential future civil-affairs projects.

Captain Balestri refined his plan by assigning two of his platoons the mission of establishing squad sized ambush positions, and one platoon, the mission of conducting information-operations patrols.

Given the immediacy of the mission, (2 soldiers of the MP battalion had been killed 2 days before), Captain Balestri issued his orders verbally to his platoon.

In order to leverage their knowledge of the local area, Captain Balestri arranged for his platoons to conduct their initial missions "jointly" with elements of the 223rd Military Police Company. The 223rd had been assigned to the area around Abu Ghraib prison for several months, and was familiar with the surrounding area.

Captain Balestri viewed the pairing of his elements with the 223rd as a way to mitigate the potential of their squads becoming misoriented in the unfamiliar terrain at night. Additionally, this would allow his platoons the ability to focus on their preparations on the establishment of the ambush positions, rather than on developing infiltration and extraction routes.

The third platoon leader, 2nd Lt. Tim Sikora and his platoon sergeant SFC David Jaeckel, were given the mission to establish counter-mortar ambush positions in an area south of the prison. Their plan was to accomplish this by splitting the platoon into two elements, one led by Lt. Sikora, the other by SFC Jaeckel. Sgt. Baddick was assigned as a rifle squad leader in the second squad of 3rd platoon/A/1-504th PIR.

Prior to both units staging for the mission, Keith Harned reported that as the soldiers of the 223rd Military Police were awaiting word to move out to meet with elements of the 82nd Airborne Division, a mortar round landed approximately 30 feet away. Luckily, there was a high wall between them and the blast. At that time, members of the 223rd became battle ready and immediately headed out to rendezvous with the 82nd.

At approximately 2100 hrs., a convoy of 5 vehicles (2 from the 223rd and 3 from the 504th PIR) began their joint ambush patrol. Sgt. A.J. Baddick was travelling in the third vehicle of the convoy of humvees, followed by his squad leader, Sgt. William Hutt, in the fourth vehicle, and SFC Jaeckel in the fifth vehicle.

The route they were taking went from Abu Ghraib prison onto Highway 1, and turned off onto a dirt road that paralleled an irrigation canal south and east of the prison. As the first humvee attempted to climb an embankment that ran alongside the canal, it slid off the embankment and into a muddy field. The second vehicle attemted to maneuver around this vehicle and up the embankment. As it did so, the driver overshot, and put the humvee into the canal."

I was told by Captain Belestri, that the canal was approximately twelve feet deep and flowing very fast. He likened it to putting your arm out of the window of a car going seventy miles per hour. He said it was very deceiving because looking at the water on the surface it appeared quite calm, but put your arm in and you couldn't keep it still.

All four soldiers inside the humvee were able to get free, but were being swept downstream by the current, and were still wearing their individual equipment and Interceptor Body Armor.

Sgt Baddick saw what was happening and immediately stopped his vehicle to provide assistance. Sgt. Baddick had extensive experience as a river guide, and likely felt more than qualified to provide rescue assistance.

Sgt. Baddick was joined by SSG. Hutt, and the two began lighting the area with flashlights and the TAC lights on their weapons. SSG. Hutt was told by the remaining MP's that there were four soldiers in the humvee, and observed that two of them were able to swim to the sides of the canal by themselves. By the time SFC Jaeckel had moved forward to the accident scene from the rear vehicle, Sgt. Baddick and SSG. Hutt had already removed their equipment and IBA, and were preparing to enter the water to assist the remaining occupants of the humvee.

In the dim light SSg. Hutt and Sgt. Baddick observed one soldier struggling in the water to stay afloat. Sgt. Baddick immediately entered the water in a move to rescue the struggling soldier.

According to SFC Jaeckel, after observing what was happening, he moved to the bridge, because the strong current was pushing Sgt. Baddick and the struggling soldier toward it. When SFC Jaeckel arrived on the bridge, one MP was below him so he reached out his hands, but could only grab his fingers, (this soldier would turn out to be Sgt. Darrin Potter). The current and the weight of the MP's equipment pulled him out of SFC Jaeckel's grasp and below the surface of the water.

Seconds later, Sgt. Baddick arrived at the bridge with the other soldier. SFC Jaeckel yelled for help and was assisted by PFC Ben Dellinger and SPC Elisah Lincoln in pulling the exhausted soldier to safety. SFC Jaeckel then told Sgt. Baddick that one MP went under the water right below him and Sgt. Baddick replied, "I got him." He dove in and didn't resurface. Sgt. Jackel and some other soldiers went to the opposite side of the bridge to see if they would come out, but never did.

After Sgt. Baddick and Sgt. Potter failed to surface on the other side of the bridge, the remaining personnel on scene began to search downstream.

Word was sent out to headquarters that they had soldiers missing. Back at Camp Mercury, Captain Belestri immediately called for two helicopters to start patrolling on each side of the canal. Additional troopers were deployed to start searching the canal in both directions. Captain Belestri told us that he feared A.J. may have been swept downstream of the accident location and was without a weapon. Scuba divers were brought in from the Air Force Para-Rescue and Special Forces teams to assist.

As it became increasingly apparent that both soldiers had been pulled underwater and swept under the bridge by the current, the Alpha Company First Sergeant, 1SG. Donald Gaines, sent an element upstream to determine if there was a valve that controlled the water's flow rate.

A squad from 3rd platoon/A/1-504 located a valve and turned it off, which slowed the water. Hours later, Sgt. Darrin Potter's body was found approximately 150 meters from the accident scene and Sgt. A.J. Baddick's body was found further downstream, a distance of approximately one kilometer, near a bridge that passes over Highway 10, on the other side of the Abu Ghraib prison."

Sgt. Major Hacker recalled the night A.J. died, saying that he was one of the first people to be notified of the incident, back at Camp Mercury. He said the chaplain was on hand and they were praying that they would find A.J. alive.

Their prayers would not be answered that night, and Sgt. Major Hacker would attend the memorial service in honor of my son. He said he would never forget the day that A.J. first entered his office asking to become a devil like his dad was.

I also had the opportunity to speak with Sgt. Michael Wright, of New York, who was a PFC in A.J.'s unit, at the time of the incident. He said he was a good friend of my son, and that he recalled the time they went out to celebrate their birthdays together at Hooters. Michael said that Hooters had a challenge where you had to eat their signature hot wings with a super hot sauce, but before you could eat them, you had to sign a waiver, releasing them of any responsibility. Michael said A.J. did it, and I remembered him telling me about it on the phone. He must have inherited that trait from my father, who had an iron gut, because I certainly am not an aficionado of super hot food.

Sgt. Wright recalled the night they went out from Camp Mercury to Abu Ghraib Prison, to help the Kentucky National Guard set up an ambush. He said they crossed over Highway 1 and headed toward the canal. They were supposed to drive along the top of the canal but ten minutes into the mission, one of the humvees went into the canal. He said he remembered seeing the humvee go straight up into the air. Then he saw A.J. dismount and head straight toward the canal. He noticed most of the guys just standing around but A.J. went straight in. He remembered watching A.J. rescue the first soldier, and then Sgt. Jaeckel yelling that he had lost his grip on the other MP, and A.J. going into the culvert after him. They didn't see them come out the other side, so he, Ben Dellinger, Peterson, Humphreys, and some others began running up and down the canal yelling for A.J. They continued this all night long in hopes of finding their missing comrade. The next morning they found him, but it was too late. Sgt. Wright assisted in pulling A.J.'s body from the canal.

On October 23rd, Sgt. Michael Wright was on a mission near Abu Ghraib to drop off snipers, not far from where A.J. had died. He said they went to a house where they stopped all the time to ask questions, bring candy, and stay in touch with the locals. Approximately 20 feet from the house, two improvised explosives detonated, and "my whole world changed", said Sgt. Wright. He lost half his left shoulder, and his patella (kneecap), was shattered. They recovered his shoulder with the AA patch still attached. He was told that he flatlined in the surgical unit. Sgt. Wright would spend the next year at Walter Reed Medical Center and return to the 82nd Airborne Division. He is planning on taking a medical discharge and moving to Orlando, Florida, to study forensics. I wish him all the best in his future endeavors.

I asked him what one thing he remembered about A.J. the most and his response was, "he was cool, real cool. When he came down from Headquarters Company, we all thought he'd be a tight-assed sergeant, but not him. He wasn't into all the political stuff that goes on. He always looked out for his guys. He was just cool, real cool."

I received information from a close friend of A.J.'s, SFC Johnathan Elliott, from Guymon, Oklahoma. Johnathan first met A.J. when he was an E-5 living in the same apartment complex in Fayetteville. He said A.J. was a driver at Division Headquarters at the time, just before Johnathan deployed to Afghanistan. He said he played cards with A.J. and drank some beers, but didn't really get to know him then. He remembers returning from Afghanistan in 2003, and at that time, he says A.J. was promoted to E-5.

This was around the time A.J. found himself a new home with the 504th. Johnathan said A.J. was assigned to A. Co. 1/504th, 3rd platoon as his Bravo Team Squad Leader. They knew they were going to deploy, so during the training they worked very hard, and A.J. was always there, pushing hard. He made some mistakes at first, but he learned fast and moved on. They deployed to Iraq in August of 2003 and travelled from Ft. Bragg to Dover, Delaware. Then on to Frankfurt, Germany and finally to Kuwait where they spent one week before being issued company vehicles to drive to their new Area of Operations, Camp Mercury, just west of Baghdad. The company commander had them put together a detail to drive the vehicles into Iraq, because they were not all travelling by truck. Four NCO's and 12 soldiers from the company were to handle the convoy. A.J. was one of the 4 NCO's to go with the vehicles because he had more humvee experience than most of them and he wanted to go.

Johnathan stated that A.J. did a good job in Iraq, he handled his men well, and was well liked by everyone. He said A.J. was a joker (what a surprise). They had non-alcoholic "near beer" in the chow hall, and A.J. would have one and pretend to be drunk, and he would get the guys laughing. One time he stripped naked and was running around the base in his boots, helmet, and a smile. A.J. liked to play cards, so he and some of the guys had a running game going. They'd be out on patrol and have their cards in their pockets, because they wouldn't leave them on the table when they went outside the wire.

The night that A.J. died, half the platoon stayed inside the wire and the other half went out. Johnathan wasn't there that night because he was inside the Abu Ghraib Prison with dysentery, and the medics wouldn't clear him to go out. He still deals with guilty feelings that he wasn't out there with his men the night of the incident.

Johnathan said that approximately 2200 hrs., two trucks came back to the prison and the rest of the platoon loaded up and went out to try to find A.J. and Sgt. Darrin Potter. He said they got to the incident site and started walking along the canal using spotlights and flashlights, yelling for them.

They searched the rest of the night until the next morning and found Darrin Potter's body, but no sign of A.J. At sun up, the Air Force sent out a team of rescue divers, and they went into the culverts under the road and found A.J.'s body. He had a wound on his head that was most likely from when he got sucked into the culvert. His body was stuck in the next culvert down from where he went under the first bridge.

Johnathan went down into the canal and helped carry A.J.'s body up to the medic vehicle that was standing by. He had been in the water approximately 12 hours at that point. Johnathan stated, "I know you wanted to see A.J.'s body, and had some issues with the Army not allowing you to view him, but I saw him and I remember it all the time. Twelve hours in the water and a nasty cut on his face, I think the Army did you a favor. Sgt. A.J. Baddick died trying to save another soldier, he was a paratrooper, and he did his job."

BAD NEWS

Chapter 10

It was October 1st, 2003. My wife, Sheila and I were sleeping soundly when the telephone woke us at approximately one o'clock in the morning. I was about to receive the phone call every parent dreads. It was my daughter, Elizabeth, and from the sound of her voice I could tell something was wrong. "Dad", she said, "A.J. is dead." My voice trembling, I said, "what?" "He's dead, A.J.'s dead." Even though I knew this was my daughter speaking to me, something in the back of my mind was telling me this could not possibly be true.

A voice I did not recognize now spoke to me. "Mr. Baddick, I am the chaplain assigned as liaison in this matter and it appears there was an accident involving your son Andrew and he drowned." I told him, "that can't be, my son was an expert swimmer." I told the chaplain there had to be a mistake, were they absolutely sure it was A.J.? He said he was sorry but it was confirmed that it was A.J. who died in the incident. My mind went blank, I dropped to the floor crying, sitting against the bed, a lost soul in a lost world. Everything came to a screeching halt, like you sometimes see in the movies, where time stands still. I just sat there and sat there, oblivious to what was going on around me. Finally, after what seemed forever, Sheila came over to me and said that she finished speaking with the chaplain and he explained that the next day a sergeant, assigned as our Casualty Affairs Liaison, would be coming to the house to meet with us. Sheila held me for a long time as I cried. She would be my life support in the coming days and weeks.

Sergeant First Class Kulikowski came to our house the following day and introduced himself as our liaison. He said he traveled from Tobyhanna Army Depot, north of us which is quite a drive. He explained to us that anything we needed or wanted information about, he was the person to go to. My first question for the sergeant was how long it would take to get our son's body back from Iraq. He told us there would first be an in depth investigation as to the cause of his death. He was right about that, it took nearly a week until A.J.'s body was flown back to the states. SFC Kulikowski also broke the news to us that A.J.'s funeral was going to be closed casket. I asked why, since the cause of his death was drowning, but the sergeant could not answer that question for us. His body arrived at Dover Air Force Base in Delaware and was now in the hands of a mortuary officer there. He called us and said we could make arrangements to have A.J.'s body released to our own funeral director. I made a phone call to the E. Franklin Griffiths funeral home in Tamaqua. I spoke to the director "Sanky" who was a personal friend of our family. My father and his were very good friends back in the day.

When Sank's father passed away he inherited his father's funeral business. Sanky had buried my father the previous year in January of 2002. He would bury my son in October of 2003, and my mother in January of 2004. Within a three year period, I would lay to rest three family members I loved dearly. Sanky came to the house and we discussed funeral arrangements for A.J. My daughter, Elizabeth, reminded me of what A.J. had said if anything should happen to him. I remembered him telling me that he wanted to be buried in Arlington but I was considering having him interred at Fort Indiantown Gap National Cemetery since it was much closer for us to visit. The rest of the family insisted I respect A.J.'s wish and have his burial at Arlington National Cemetery. I finally decided that if A.J. wanted to be laid to rest there, then I had to follow through with it or I would regret it later on. Sanky said he would take care of the arrangements with Arlington, and much to our despair, he found out that A.J. could not be buried there for about a month because they were backed up with funerals. The following day, Sanky called us and said he received a phone call from the lady at Arlington who told him they would be able to accommodate us and have A.J. buried within the next few days. We were so relieved to hear the news.

Word of A.J.'s death spread quickly through the Jim Thorpe area, where he worked as a guide for Jim Thorpe River Adventures during high school and after graduation. Then-owner Dave Kuhn had met A.J. when he was twelve years old and took his first trip on the Lehigh River. Two years later, Kuhn said A.J. was a proficient kayaker. Kuhn said A.J., who called him "Uncle Dave," worked on and off for him for thirteen years. He said he had an easygoing personality and was well-liked by customers whom he guided down the river. Flags were flown at half-mast at the Jim Thorpe area schools, the Carbon County courthouse, and the Dolan-Jones-Martino American Legion Post 304 on the east side of Jim Thorpe, not far from A.J.'s home.

"He was always willing to help other individuals without thinking of himself first," said Bill Zahora, who taught A.J. during his freshman year at Jim Thorpe Area Senior High School. "Even in the end he was trying to help another person. He wasn't selfish in any way, and he was always willing to give of himself." An outgoing student, Zahora said that A.J. was a difficult student to forget. "He was always yelling 'hello' from way down the hallway. He had so much enthusiasm and class. He was very outgoing and unique."

Zahora said that A.J., a 1997 graduate, had a "big smile on his face" when he told his teachers that he would be entering the military. "He was so thrilled that he was going to be serving his country," he said. "He really loved the military." Zahora said, "It was a pleasure to know him, he may be gone, but he is certainly not forgotten."

Ed Glassic, who was chaplain for the Jim Thorpe American Legion, said he talked to A.J. just before he left for Iraq. "He was in the Legion just before he left," Glassic recalled. "I remember as he left, my wife told him to 'be careful' and that's the last we saw him." Glassic remembered A.J. as someone who was very approachable. "Everyone liked him, he was very nonchalant," he said.

"He would do anything for you, and he loved being in the service."

Charles McHugh, then-director of the Carbon County Office of Veteran's Affairs, said, "I knew him all his life, I watched him grow up." McHugh said A.J. would visit him during his leaves from the service and that he wanted to make a career out of the service. "All he wanted to do was be in the Army and be a paratrooper." McHugh was upset by A.J.'s death. "When you lose one in your own hometown, your home county, it's tough to take," he said. "A.J. was one hell of a soldier."

William J. Davis, a teacher at Jim Thorpe High School had this to say about A.J.: "A.J. Baddick was a heroic young man who I will always remember as the bright, happy, enthusiastic kid in my twelfth grade English Class. A.J. would do anything to help me, and I knew immediately he was a young man I could trust. A.J. knew I was a veteran and he asked me many questions about the Army. A.J. told me he wanted to be a combat infantryman, and then earn his airborne wings. He fulfilled his destiny and much more. I am extremely proud to have known him and right next to the flag in my classroom, is a picture of A.J. Baddick, a true American Hero."

Rosemary Karper of Jim Thorpe said, "A.J. is a true hero. If it was not for him talking me into the military, I would not be serving in the United States Air Force. A.J. was a good friend, always willing to help out when in need. A good guy who listened to your problems. I am so proud of him for giving his life for the freedom of this great country."

Alicia Matukonis said, "A.J. is one of my angels in heaven, watching over me. I know he is happy and having fun up there with his best friend Kevin, who passed away a few years earlier. I grew up with A.J. and worked with him at the whitewater rafting company. He LOVED the water. He was the best guide on the river because he cared so much about everyone's safety, but he still knew how to have a good time out there. I'll never forget him pulling me up onto his kayak to save me when I got tossed overboard by my friends. A.J. was an amazing guy and everyone in town was so proud of him for what he was doing. I'm so glad that the last time I saw him I told him I was proud of him and gave him a hug. He is a true American Hero. I miss you A.J."

Jamie Crowley had this to say: "I went to school with A.J. and graduated with him. He was a great guy. He even taught me how to drive with his mom's old car. His mother didn't know he was using her car to teach me. He loved to take me to Leisureland because he knew the cops would not be around. He even taught me how to get through life and not worry about what other people said. We did so much stuff together as friends, I'm really going to miss him. I also feel so bad for his mother, he always talked good about her. I'm going to miss this person that touched my life in a special way. Love Jamie, I'll miss you A.J."

Sanky Griffith also made arrangements for my son's viewing. It was held on October 9, 2003, at Saint Joseph's Roman Catholic Church in Jim Thorpe, Pennsylvania. I personally have never seen so many flowers or people at a wake before. We stood at the front of the church where my son's casket was and the people just kept coming and coming to offer their condolences to the point where I was near exhaustion. Kevin Trice's mother and father came up to console us and with tears in her eyes, Nancy said, "it's good to know Kevin and A.J. are together again." I replied, "yes, and probably raising hell in heaven."

There were two officers, a captain and a lieutenant, from Fort Hood, Texas, who had been A.J.'s previous commanders and they introduced themselves to me and Sheila. These two men could not say enough about what a dedicated and professional soldier A.J. had been. There were soldiers from the 82nd Airborne at Fort Bragg. There was a soldier who was a personal friend of A.J.'s, Staff Sergeant Gary LeLeux who was in the 101st Airborne Division. He was from Louisiana, and he and my son met years earlier while they were stationed at Fort Hood, Texas. They ended up bumping into one another in Afghanistan. Gary was on an observation post in the mountains of Afghanistan when they noticed insurgents setting up a mortar for an ambush.

After calling his superiors, they were told to open fire on the enemy. In the ensuing firefight, insurgents turned the mortar around and fired some rounds in Sgt. LeLeux's direction, wounding him with pieces of shrapnel. They did, however, silence the mortar position for good. Gary spoke with A.J. the day he was leaving to go to Iraq. "A.J. called me at my house." He told me to "take it easy" and I said, "be careful."

After A.J.'s funeral service, Gary asked if he could have a few words with me. We went to the parking lot and with tears in his eyes, he confessed to me that he felt it was his fault that A.J. re-enlisted, because he told A.J. he was going to jump school and airborne. I told Gary to put his mind at ease. I explained how I had been in the 82nd Airborne and A.J. re-enlisted on the condition that they send him to the 82nd also. I told Gary that A.J. was made for the military, that he loved it, and that he had plans on going to Ranger School when he got back from Iraq. I said, "look Gary, A.J. would have made a career out of the army, you had nothing to do with his decision." I sensed a sigh of relief and hoped I had put aside any grief he had been feeling.

There were family members, friends I hadn't seen in years, and people I didn't even know. The line to enter the church was so long the funeral director suggested we stop it at some point or it would go on all night. The line was, in fact, cut off, to the disappointment of many, many people and apologies were made. Someone made a comment to me that it would be a good night to rob Jim Thorpe, because everyone was here. Soldiers that had traveled many miles to accompany A.J.'s body were getting tired so it was suggested that his body be taken back to the funeral home overnight. We had been assured by Sanky, the funeral director, that his casket would be securely locked in a room till morning. We agreed that was the best plan of action to give the soldiers a much deserved nights rest.

The next day, October 10, 2003, was A.J.'s funeral service at St. Joseph's Church. When we arrived, once again there was a sea of people. Prior to the start of the service, U.S. Congressman Paul Kanjorski presented a flag that was flown over the United States Capitol building in memory of A.J. The funeral service was beautifully done by the Reverend Francis Baransky, pastor of St. Joseph's Church, who reminded everyone during his sermon, "greater love than this, no one has, that one lay down his life for his friends."   Concelebrants for the service were the Reverend Richard Clement of Reading, Monsignor John Chismar from Immaculate Conception Church in Jim Thorpe, and the Reverend Joseph Whalen of Pottsville. Father Clement was pastor of the church we attended and Father Whalen had been the chaplain at the State Correctional Institution in Mahanoy, where I worked.

As I sat in the church pew and listened to what everyone had to say about my son, it suddenly occurred to me that I had not said anything about him. It was right near the end of the service that something came over me, and as the funeral director came up the side aisle to end things, I stood up and looked at him. Sanky stopped and gave me a wave as if to say, "The floor is yours." I am by no means a comfortable person when it comes to public speaking, but I felt an overwhelming need to speak some words about my son. My wife, Sheila, looked up at me with a puzzled look on her face. I exited the pew and made my way to the altar, placing my hand on A.J.'s casket as I passed. I took out my reading glasses, and as I did, I thanked all those who had attended our son's viewing and the funeral service that day.

It was very hard to speak, but I began by reading an email from my niece, Christine Kinney, and in it she said, "Dear Uncle Joe, I have very few words that can offer any comfort other than that I am so proud of A.J. I am so honored to have known and loved him. It gives me great comfort to know that people like him, with fearless honor, protect us every day."

I then spoke of a television program my mother and I were watching about angels. A gentleman by the name of Dr. Margolies of the University of Kansas said that angels are a part of us. We believe an angel is a being that does something good for another being. "If that is the case, I said, then I believe that A.J. is now an angel."

I told of how we received a sympathy card from a co-worker of mine by the name of Janice Steinhart. Inside the card she wrote, "your son was a very special person and you can take comfort in knowing you were given the opportunity to have an angel in your family. Someone who lays down his life for a friend or comrade is truly God's angel."

I finished by saying, "I know that my son not only earned his earthly wings but also his heavenly wings. A.J. my son, you are truly airborne."

As I returned to the seat next to Sheila, she leaned over and gave me a kiss. I looked at the altar and on each side were two life size angels. I said to Sheila, "they made me do it." She said, "Who?" I pointed to the angels and said, "the angels." I knew then that a heavenly force got me to my feet to speak about my son, and I was so glad I did.

As the funeral service concluded, we filed out of the pews and followed our son's casket to the rear of the church. We waited as the funeral director readied the casket for the transition onto a horse drawn caisson. I looked to my immediate left and saw some of my very good friends from the Department of Corrections in their dress uniforms and mouthed, "thank you." As we stood there, all of a sudden, it seemed as if the church floor dropped a few inches and we all gazed at one another wondering what happened. My mom said, "Did you feel that?" I told her, "Yeah, I hope it holds up till we get out of here." Perhaps with the church at overflow capacity it was telling us that the weight was too much to bear for an old structure, such as it was. Afterwards, someone would remark that A.J. kept the floor from collapsing, that he held it up. Six pallbearers, all in the military, and all friends of A.J.'s, carried his casket outside. Waiting out in front of the church was a caisson with two black horses in front. Two men in black suits and stovepipe hats sat atop the caisson. Once A.J.'s casket was outside on the caisson, we exited the church to our respective cars. Outside the church the Jim Thorpe Fire Department had erected high ladders on either side of the street and stretched across was a black banner signifying that one of their own had passed away. John McCabe of Effort Pennsylvania, a member of the Pocono Mountain Regional Pipe and Drum Corps, while in his full dress uniform, played "Amazing Grace" on his bagpipe as the caisson pulled away from Saint Joseph's Church. With the sun shining brightly and a breeze snapping the flags held aloft by local veterans, the caisson proceeded down North Street under the arch created by the Jim Thorpe Fire Department. It traveled down North Street and turned left onto Front Street where it passed by A.J.'s home. A.J.'s kayak had been placed in front of the house as a silent tribute to the fallen soldier along with a sign that read, "Pray for Our Soldiers." On the next door neighbor's porch hung a sign that read, "A.J.

Our Hero, You Will Be Missed, But Not 4 Gotten." The procession rounded the corner onto Center Street and headed north to the Fairview Hose Company, where A.J.'s casket was removed from the caisson and loaded into the hearse for transport back to the E. Franklin Griffith's Funeral Home to await burial in Arlington National Cemetery.

ARLINGTON

Chapter 11

I awoke the morning of October 14, 2003 and thought, "Today we lay our son to rest in Arlington, Virginia." It seemed as if I was in a dream, a bad dream. Parents are not supposed to bury their children. We're supposed to grow old and die, and they bury us. How could I be in such a convoluted situation? That Tuesday was not a particularly nice day weather-wise. I remember it being cold and damp. As Sheila and I began getting ready for yet another very difficult day in our lives, my mind started drifting to happier days with my son. It was just too hard to believe it was over. All the stress and depression of the last few days had taken its toll on me, my body decided to remind me just how low my resistance had become. As I began to put on my underwear, I threw out my back. I could hardly straighten up or move. I thought, "This is just great, how am I going to manage getting through this day?" Sheila said she would call my cousin, Dr. Peter Baddick, and see what he thought. We had contracted a bus to take our family and friends to Arlington and Pete would be on the bus. He told Sheila he would bring the necessary medication I would need to get me through the day. I finally managed to get dressed, with Sheila's help, and we went to the funeral home. We got on the bus and Dr. Pete was there waiting to medicate me. All I remember him saying was, "take this, and this, and this, and this." I must admit, when we arrived at Arlington, I felt much better. With the aid of a cane I was moving around pretty good.

I started reminiscing about the time I brought A.J. and Elizabeth to Washington for a visit. I remember we did a lot of walking and I showed them the Washington Monument, and we went to the Smithsonian Museum of Natural History. Then we went over to Arlington and I know A.J. was impressed. However, on the ride home, I asked him what he enjoyed the most, and his answer was, "the pigeons."

We arrived at Arlington early and some of our friends wanted to see the Tomb of the Unknown Soldier. I made the long walk up the hill and we were in time to see the changing of the guard ceremony. My godchild, Chelsea Mizenko, was really excited to be able to view the entire procedure. We went to President John F. Kennedy's gravesite and then back down the hill to the Administration Building. Outside there were eight paratroopers from the 82nd Airborne Division, and by the flash on their berets I could see they were members of Headquarters and Headquarters Company. I went over and introduced myself and Sheila to them. I told them our son was being buried there that day. The man in charge, First Sergeant Miller, told us they knew, they were there for A.J. He explained that they had served with A.J. in

Afghanistan. I shook each soldier's hand and thanked them for being there.

We then headed over to Section 60, where our son would be interred with full military honors. Nothing can prepare you when you look at the hole in the ground, and know, that is where you are about to place your son's body for eternity. It had been drizzling off and on and it was cold, so very cold and damp. The service was presided over by Chaplain, Lt. Colonel Joseph Gouderau. Off in the distance a lone bugler blew taps. Members of the 3rd Infantry Division, "The Old Guard", fired a twenty one gun salute. They performed their duties with precision and professionalism befitting a fallen comrade. General Richard Rowe, Rear Detachment Commander of the 82nd Airborne Division, took the folded flag and presented it to A.J.'s mother. He then took another folded flag, touched it to my son's coffin, and presented it to me. He then shook my hand, and in his hand was his personal challenge coin. We looked into each other's eyes and knew the importance of the exchange without the need for words. At the end of the service, we each went forward and placed a rose on A.J.'s coffin. The hardest part for me was watching my mother place her rose on her grandson's coffin. It seemed so unnatural.

We then were ushered back to what is referred to as the columbarium. It was here that General Rowe presented us with A.J.'s Bronze Star and a beautiful wooden case to house our flags. Later on A.J. would receive the Soldier's Medal, which is given for saving another soldier's life. A.J. got his wish, to be buried among all those brave warriors. He was the thirtieth American soldier killed in Operation

Iraqi Freedom to be buried in Arlington. Andrew was not the first Baddick to die in a combat related circumstance. Two of our cousins died in World War II. One was John "Mickey" Baddick of Tamaqua and the other was Jacob "Kuba" Baddick of Trescow. Andrew also came from a family of previous airborne troopers. Aside from myself, we had an uncle, Edward Baddick, my dad's brother, who was a member of the 11th Airborne Division during World War II. He saw action in the Phillipines at Leyte and also on New Guinea.

We thanked everyone and said our goodbyes, then loaded on the bus for the long ride home. There were also two bus loads of people from Jim Thorpe. As the bus made the long turn around Arlington, I couldn't help but think about all those headstones, and under each and every one there lays the body of person who gave their life for their beloved country. I think it would be a good thing to load all the young people of this generation on buses and drive them through Arlington National Cemetery to show them that freedom doesn't fall from the sky into their laps. Our freedom has been paid for by all those brave warriors who now reside in Arlington, and at a very high price. And it's not just the young people who need to see it, it's also the Barbara Streisands, and the Alec Baldwins, the Michael Moores, and Robert Redfords and Rosie O'Donnells. All those Hollywood types that are so out of touch with reality, because they don't live in the real world. I have met many of the men and women serving in our armed forces today, and this country can be proud of how professional and dedicated they are. They are some of the finest our country has to offer. May God bless them all for the outstanding jobs they do.

Thomas Peske is the Public Affairs Specialist for the United States Army in the Military District of Washington. He's a civilian who works for the Army. He probably attends more funerals than most funeral directors. Peske's duties include assisting and controlling the visiting press who come to Arlington to cover a burial. No interviews with family members are allowed in Arlington, and Peske works hard to see that rule is obeyed. "We want to protect their (the family's) privacy. Certain areas are set aside from the actual burial site for the press to observe and take photographs. Most funerals are innocuous to Peske, who sometimes observes more than two dozen a week. However, A.J.'s funeral didn't fall into that category. Although he didn't know the family, he knew about Jim Thorpe. "I've visited there and a few years ago I went white water rafting there, on the Lehigh River." It's ironic that the man helping to coordinate the burial of a young soldier who lived two hundred and fifty miles away should have something in common.

Some of my son's happiest times were spent on the Lehigh, in his kayak, guiding trips down the river. Who knows, perhaps Thomas Peske and A.J. ran into one another without even knowing it. Fate is strange that way.

Just what is Arlington National Cemetery? Best known of the more than one hundred national cemeteries in the United States, Arlington's green slopes shelter veterans from every war that has involved our nation. Over 275,000 service men and women, and their family members rest on the 624 acres of Virginia land.

Approximately twenty four burials are conducted every weekday.

All who are remembered there have this in common: service to their country. To each one, no matter what rank or station, whether decorated hero or unknown, belongs a place of honor.

When Civil War casualties overflowed hospitals and burial grounds near Washington, D.C., Quartermaster General Montgomery Meigs proposed in 1864 that two hundred acres of the Robert E. Lee family property at Arlington be taken for a cemetery. "The grounds around the mansion," Meigs wrote, "are admirably adapted to such a use."

The cemetery is open year round, 365 days, for visitation. The 3rd U.S. Infantry, traditionally known as "The Old Guard" is the Army's official ceremonial unit and escort to the president. It is the oldest active duty unit in the Army, serving our nation since 1784.

A funeral with full military honors is a dignified and moving experience. An honor guard accompanies the American flag-draped coffin. Muffled drums beat the slow cadence as the coffin is carried to the gravesite. Before the remains are lowered, a squad fires three rifle volleys and a bugler blows the long notes of "Taps." Finally, the flag is folded and presented to the next of kin.

Many prominent figures are buried in Arlington: President John F. Kennedy, Glenn Miller, Audie Murphy (WWII Medal of Honor recipient), Joe Louis (world heavyweight boxing champ and WWII veteran), Pierre Charles L'Enfant (designer of the capital city), Admiral Richard Byrd (polar explorer and Medal of Honor recipient), Oliver Wendell Holmes (Civil War veteran and Supreme Court Justice), Lt. General Claire Chennault (organized the All Volunteer Group, The Flying Tigers), General of the Armies, John J. Pershing (WWI), and sailors from the USS Maine at Havana harbor.

Sentinels of the 3rd U.S. Infantry maintain an around the clock vigil at the Tomb of the Unknowns. A sentinel paces 21 steps down the mat before the tomb, pauses 21 seconds, and returns. The changing of the guard takes place every hour (or half-hour from April through September). Entombed here are the remains of unknown servicemen from World War I, World War II, Korea, and Vietnam. "Here rests in honored glory an American soldier known but to God" reads the inscription on the sarcophagus of the World War I soldier entombed there in 1921.

Symbols of human struggle and sacrifice, the stones and monuments of Arlington National Cemetery are steeped in history. In their time, all who are buried there - taken from many walks of life, creeds, and races - answered their country's call. Their stories will forever be remembered.

Inscribed inside the apse of the Memorial Amphitheater are these words, taken from a letter, written June 26, 1775, by then General George Washington, to the Provincial Congress. "When we assumed the soldier, we did not lay aside the citizen." Inscribed above the stage, from Abraham Lincoln's Gettysburg Address, it reads, "We here highly resolve that these dead shall not have died in vain."

As the bus pulled away from Arlington National Cemetery, I went to the front of the bus and asked the driver for the microphone. I thanked everyone for coming on the trip and let them know that I didn't want the trip home to be depressing. Now that we had buried my son, I thought it only befitting that we toast to A.J., as I knew he would approve. I explained that on the past Father's Day, A.J. had bought me a beer stein and a brandy snifter with the 504th Parachute Infantry Regiment logo on them. I said that I had brought along some Windsor Canadian to put in the brandy snifter and soda to put in the beer stein for the non alcohol drinkers. I asked everyone to take a drink in honor of my son. My mother and my Aunt Helen Campbell were sitting in the first seat. To my utter amazement, my mother, not much of a drinker, asked me for the brandy snifter. I said, "Mom, it has whiskey in it." She replied, "That's okay, it's for my grandson." And with that she took a hearty drink. Aunt Helen opted for the soda. The two goblets were passed all around the bus. Then, my cousin, JoAnn Paslawsky, A.J.'s godmother, had thought about a fitting tribute to Sgt. A.J. Baddick, who loved life and a good time as much as anyone. How about a hot baloney toast? "A.J. loved hot baloney, so my sister Jean made some over the weekend so they would be ready for the trip." She said, "We hammered them on the way home. I was dipping them out of the jar. That got harder as the jar emptied, because I was using a dinky little plastic fork." There was plenty to eat and drink.

Then, my cousin, Dr. Pete, had brought along a CD player and asked the bus driver if he could pipe the music through the microphone. The driver agreed that it would be alright and Pete played Lee Greenwood's "Proud to Be an American." Everyone was singing; I tried to but I'd just start crying and couldn't do it. It was a most memorable trip home thanks to our family and good friends.

VALOR

A.J.'s Godmother, JoAnn, sent us a copy of a letter she wrote to the editor of The Catholic Standard & Times. It follows:

> "To the Editor: Please extend my thanks to Gloria Pinsker and your layout artist for this week's installment on the series about the Apostles.
>
> Wednesday evening I found out that my godson, U.S. Army Sergeant Andrew Joseph Baddick, died in Iraq. He was attempting to rescue other military personnel trapped inside a vehicle that had crashed into a canal with a very strong current. The irony is that Andrew had always been a strong swimmer and had done many water rescues while working for a white water rafting company on the Lehigh River.

Thursday evening I could barely see. I hadn't slept the night before, and my eyes were tired and swollen from crying. Nevertheless, I decided to try and read The Catholic Standard & Times. I am so glad that I did. I only got as far as Gloria's article but I can't explain the peace that came to me as I read the headline and the subheading, 'Ordinary Men, Extraordinary Lives, Spritual Lessons from the Apostles'......In (Andrew's) strong, quiet, solid character, we see a shining example of the humility that acknowledges that God can accomplish great good through those who do not care who receives the recognition.

After reading the rest of the information in the article about Andrew, the Apostle, I realized just how well my godson wore his name! It was then that I realized why God had called him back to himself although he was still a young man. Thank you for helping me in my grief."

-JoAnn Paslawsky"

In her article, Gloria Pinsker wrote of the Apostle Andrew:

"Before meeting Jesus, Andrew and his younger brother Simon Peter, along with James and John, were partners in a fishing business. Andrew and John were disciples of John the Baptist; they were the first to follow Jesus when the Baptist pointed

Him out as "the Lamb of God." Later, Andrew brought Simon Peter to Jesus. Yet although Peter, James, and John became part of the Lord's inner circle, and granted special confidences and privileges, Andrew did not. I often wonder how he felt about this. Was he hurt? Did he struggle to rise above jealousy and envy? Being human, he probably did.

Although perhaps not so strong a leader as his brother, Andrew was active in bringing others to Christ. In contrast to the bemused Philip, he was resourceful enough to tell Jesus about the boy who had the loaves and fishes. Andrew also helped the hesitant Philip inform Jesus that a group of Greeks wanted to meet him. (Jn 12:20-22). This suggests that Andrew understood Jesus' call to save all people, not just the Jews. It's a safe bet that Andrew was a strong organizer and administrator among the Apostles.

Andrew inspires us to lead others to Christ and to conquer envy and jealousy in order to serve the greater good. In his strong, quiet, solid character, we see a shining example of the humility that acknowledges those who do not care who receives the recognition."

Gloria Pinsker sent a reply to my cousin JoAnn:

"I once read that St. Andrew was known for his valor during storms at sea. Being a fisherman, he lived much of his life around water, just as your godson did. Your godson was a true hero. I feel certain that St. Andrew was very near to his namesake during his time of need, and they are now enjoying one another's company in heaven. We are all here on earth for a unique purpose, and when that purpose is fulfilled, we are free to go Home, where each of us ultimately belongs. It is difficult for those of us left behind on earth when loved ones die, but knowing in our hearts that they have accomplished what they were put here to do is a great comfort in our loss.

That the layout artist chose to highlight a sentence about Andrew, and that you, who had just lost a godson named Andrew, would happen to see it on the very day you needed it most, is something only the most hardened cynic could call mere "coincidence." Although I have witnessed over and over God's wonderful synchronicity in bringing the right things into our lives at just the right time, I am awed all over again every time it happens.

Please extend my condolences to Andrew's parents. Although their pain seems bottomless right now, they can feel justifiably proud to have raised such a selfless and courageous son. Thank you once again for so generously sharing your experience. God Bless."

I looked up St. Andrew on the internet and it says his name was taken from the Greek meaning "valor." In A.J.'s case it would certainly seem to fit. It should also be noted that St. Andrew brought his brother, Simon Peter, to Jesus. Andrew's brother would become St. Peter, first Bishop of Rome, to whom Jesus said, "you are Peter, and upon this rock, I will build my church."   That church still stands strong to this day.

A few week following A.J.'s death, Sheila and I were at Sunday mass and afterward Father Rich Clement came over to speak with us. He asked how we were doing and I said "okay". We began to talk about A.J. I said, "I guess God needed A.J. more than we did." Father Rich replied, "listen, God had nothing to do with your son's death. Do you think God took all those lives in the Twin Towers? There is evil in this world, and that is what took A.J.'s life."

When we got home I started contemplating what Father Rich had said to us. This is how I rationalized his explanation. If the insurgents, who obviously were evil, had not been firing mortar rounds into the Abu Ghraib Prison that night, A.J.'s unit would not have been sent on that ambush, resulting in his death. That works for me. It also explains how evil men took the lives of all those lost in the Twin Towers. There is no doubt there is evil all around us, all the more reason to be prepared when our time comes.

I worked at the prison with a woman by the name of Terri DelBalso, who also serves in the Army National Guard. Terri happened to be in Iraq at the time of A.J.'s death. She was with the 320th Military Police Battalion, stationed at Abu Ghraib Prison and recalled the night A.J.

died. She sent me a beautiful letter that I would like to share with you. This is the letter:

"Dear Joe,

Hello there. I hope you are doing OK. I think about you almost every day since your son was killed here. I know you are a strong man, but a tragedy like this will be the test of a lifetime. My prayers are with you and I know God is helping you through.

I recently learned that you never received the letter I wrote to you right after I returned from Andy's Memorial Service. I sent it to the address his unit gave me.....I guess I forgot you were divorced from Ann. I guess she received your letter. Well, now I have your correct address and I'll tell you what I wanted you to hear a few months ago.

I never had the pleasure of meeting Andy. Unbelievably, he lived 50 meters from where I live here at the Abu Ghraib Prison; I was gone all day and he was gone all night. If our paths ever crossed, and they may very well have, I never knew it. My loss, I have no doubt.

On the night your son was killed, we had a mortar attack here. Around that time, the 82nd had recently become part of our family at Abu Ghraib Prison to help us combat these attackers. Sgt. Baddick - Andy - was on a quick response team that was dispatched to the location believed to be the origin of the mortar fire. On the way there, a Humvee in front of the one your son was in, drove into a canal and some of the soldiers were trapped. Andy's vehicle stopped to help and, without hesitation, your son jumped into the water and was searching about. He is credited with saving the life of one of the men he pulled from the canal. When he went down for the last man who was unaccounted for, he never resurfaced. Joe, your son gave his life saving others - his brothers - and we all still mourn the loss of the life of one of our own. I'm sure you heard all this already, but, as your friend, I wanted to personally share this with you.

The next morning when I came into work, I quickly heard about the events of the night before. I glanced down on my desk and saw a report called an SIR (serious incident report) and noticed the names of the soldiers that died the night before. The first name was the second soldier your son tried to save.

The second name was just listed as "Baddick" - no first name, nothing else.

We had yet to get the details from the 82nd. Of course, my eyes were riveted to the paper. "Baddick" isn't an extremely common name.

I suddenly remembered all the stories you told me about your son Andy going to jump school, loving the Army, etc. Then, Joe, it dawned on me.

I ran over to the 82nd First Sergeant and demanded more information. He sent Andy's roommate to my office to talk to me right away - my worst fears were confirmed. I was out of commission for a little while as I was thinking about the awful news that my friend Joe was soon going to hear.

A bunch of us took the trip to the 82nd Airborne Headquarters, here in Iraq, to attend Andy's Memorial Service. It wasn't very far from Abu Ghraib Prison, maybe 25 minutes, but it seemed far. It was a wonderful service.

The entire company assembled in platoons outside. Key people spoke - Andy's roommate, the company commander, and the chaplain. I took some pictures that I will share with you when I get back to SCI-Mahanoy. When the service was over, one by one, we all walked up to the memorial set up in Andy's honor. Most saluted, some prayed, I cried. As I looked upon his helmet and boots, I told Andy that I was going to tell his father about what he did.... about how deeply we all feel the loss because, even though we may not personally know each soldier that gives his life for his country, we feel the pain of losing a brother or sister every time one of us makes that sacrifice. That day, though, I was also feeling sorrow for my friend back home who would have to deal with this tragedy for the rest of his life.

Joe, please know that my thoughts and prayers are with you. Michaelene Fanelli has written me - that's how I learned you never received my first letter - and told me you seem to be doing well. Please accept my deepest condolences at the loss of your son. Everyone who hears that someone dies in Iraq is quick to say, "he died a hero." Although that is not always the case, it is truly the case with Sgt. Andrew Baddick. He is remembered by all of us for the selfless way he jumped into that canal, not thinking of his own safety, and gave all he had to help someone else.

Take care of yourself, Joe, and be proud. Many men raise sons, but you raised a hero. See you when I get back to Mahanoy,

Your Friend, Terri."

I was to learn that Terri would once again deploy to Iraq in 2008. She would not forget A.J. on this trip back to the sandbox. Terri would have a flag flown in honor and in memory of Sgt. Andrew J. Baddick, over Forward Operating Base Cropper, Badhdad, Iraq. She had it sent to my house with a beautiful letter and a plaque. Thank you Terri, my family truly appreciates this wonderful act of kindness.

In the weeks and months to come, we would receive a huge amount of cards, letters, newspaper articles, books, flags, pictures and many other things that had something to do with A.J. There were letters of condolence from President George W. Bush, Elizabeth Dole, Donald Rumsfeld, Les Brownlee (Acting Secretary of the Army), General Swannack (82nd Airborne Division Commander), General Youngman (Kentucky National Guard Commander), Jack Tilley (12th Sergeant Major of the Army), and others.

We received flags that were flown at bases in Iraq and Afghanistan. We received a book, "American Soldier", by General Tommy Franks, with an inscription that reads, "for Sgt. A.J. Baddick - American Soldier, Patriot, Hero..... and Friend! In Memory, Tommy Franks." Also another book sent by Karl Zinsmeister, "Dawn Over Baghdad." Inside the front cover he wrote, "For the Baddick Family, in memory of Andrew - An American Hero." He was embedded with the 82nd Airborne for three months in combat areas, and mentions A.J. in his book on page 18. Friends had cut out newspaper articles about A.J. and laminated them. We had a huge Rubbermaid tub filled with stuff and I didn't know what to do with it all.

We had a spare bedroom that was more or less my room to watch golf and smoke a cigar now and then. However, Sheila's daughter, Tyna, her husband, Rick, and daughter Kaitlyn, were having their house built prior to A.J.'s death and my man cave became their room. I told Sheila that when the kids moved out I was going to have a golf mural painted on the wall and put all kinds of golf items on display. As I gave thought about what to do with all of the paraphernalia we had pertaining to A.J., an idea suddenly struck me. Why don't I turn the spare room into A.J.'s room? That's exactly what I did, and it kept me busy for awhile and was very therapeutic for me. I painted the walls light blue and put splashes of red and dark blue here and there. I put up an American flag border all around, and then I started hanging all the things I could. I framed all the letters for hanging and bought a bookcase for some of the other stuff. A.J.'s flag case and folded flag are on display with all his awards and citations. There are things hanging on the walls too numerous to mention but each one has special meaning for me. Finally, I had my man cave back and now it was so much better than before. Anytime I need a place to relax and find comfort, I go into A.J.'s room, shut the door, light up a stogie, have a Jack Daniels, and talk to my son. There is a large picture of him on the wall in front of my seat, and another one directly behind me. A wonderfully calm feeling comes over me in that special room. Funny thing; I'll ask our dog Harry (a Westie), "do you want to go up to A.J.'s room"? He's up the stairs in a flash and ready to get up on the sofa in his spot. I think he finds as much comfort in that room as I do, like he never forgot about A.J. And when I talk to Harry about A.J. he looks at me and turns his head from side to side as if he really understands what I'm saying.

Sometimes I think what a shame it is that A.J. is no longer here, to perhaps have children of his own, and carry on the Baddick name. I think that is something I would have enjoyed but will never have the chance to find out.

However, fate took a strange turn, as I will explain shortly.

One day Elizabeth was at our house and I took her upstairs to see A.J.'s room for the first time. As she looked around at all of A.J.'s stuff, she turned to me and said, "dad, I never realized what an honor it must be to be part of the 82nd Airborne." I told her that it is a very special fraternity her brother belonged to, a very proud one indeed.

At the time of A.J.'s death, Elizabeth was pregnant with her first child. I asked her if she had names picked out and she replied, "if it's a boy I'm naming him Andy, after my brother." I asked, "what if it's a girl?" She answered, "if it's a girl I'm naming her Andi after my brother." Well, it turned out to be a girl and she was named Andi Rose. Andi after her Uncle A.J. and Rose after my mother. Elizabeth would call me and tell me that Andi got into some kind of mischief and she would say that she just knew that A.J. was putting Andi up to it. Elizabeth told me that Andi Rose had a book at home to help prepare her for kindergarten. She wanted to do a Build-A-Bear, where a child makes their own bear from scratch. Her mom and dad made her a deal, that if she completed one page of the book each day and finished, they would take her to do a Build-A-Bear. Now, Elizabeth said that it took Andi a mere two minutes to complete a page. On the third day, Andi Rose blurted out, "I don't like homework, never did, never will." Keep in mind that this little girl is entering kindergarten, and never really experienced the joys of homework yet. So, Elizabeth seems to think this is a shining example of Uncle A.J. at work behind the scenes, prompting his niece on what to say. One time they were at our house and we were up in A.J.'s room and Andi told us she was talking to Uncle A.J. and that she saw him. Elizabeth and I looked at one another and I said, "I believe it, I wouldn't be a bit surprised." Every time I look at my granddaughter she reminds me that life goes on. I miss my son so much, but Andi really eases the sadness in my heart. I thank God and Elizabeth for bringing her into our lives. She just loves coming to Pappy Joe's house and playing with her cousins, Kaitlyn and Kyle, who are both Tyna's children. They get along so well, and they are a joy to have at our house. Once a month we have all three sleep over and we take them to the movies and play games. Kyle is a huge Star Wars fan and he always brings his four light sabers with him so we can battle. Of course, Pappy always loses but that is because we took the grandkids to Walt Disney World and Kyle went through the Jedi Training Academy, so he knows all the secret moves to use on me. Andi Rose is an aspiring basketball player, for she is seldom seen without a ball in her hands. She loves to dribble and shoot, even if there's no basket. Her mom and dad take her to most all of the Marian High School Fillies (girls) games. Elizabeth says all the girls pay attention to her and at half time she goes out on the court to play. It would be great to see Andi play for Marian since I played basketball there and so did Elizabeth. Only time will tell. And the oldest, Kaitlyn, we're not sure about her, she has many talents. She plays soccer, basketball, she dances, but the one talent she possesses, that she excels at, is making up stories, and we have a feeling she may one day become a writer. Kaitlyn just recently had to do a school assignment and wrote this beautiful story:

My Hero
by: Kaitlyn Dierolf

"My hero is my Uncle A.J. My uncle was a very brave and heroic person. Still, to this very day, I wish I could spend just one more day with him.

I lost my uncle in war, and this is why he's my hero. He died overnight when a hummer went over a bank and into a river. He jumped in and got one man out, but when trying to get the second man out of the car, he hit his head and drowned. I wish he hadn't gone into war, but then I couldn't say he died fighting for our freedom.

Even though I lost my uncle when I was 4, I still have faint memories of him.

The last time I can remember him is the summer of 2003. He was leaving for Iraq and wanted a hug and a kiss, I gave him neither. I used to feel bad because I didn't say goodbye, but I know he loved me as much as I love him. Years have passed and his sister, my aunt, has a girl named Andi. She is now having a boy named T.J. Even though he never met Andi or T.J., and hardly met Kyle, he would have loved to be an uncle of 4.

My uncle sacrificed, fought, and lost his life in war. Not many people know who died for their country. I know one, my uncle. Even though he didn't die in battle, that doesn't mean he's not a hero. In my mind, everyone who served, and who is now fighting, is a hero. Freedom is not free, Because it comes with a cost."

Kaitlyn certainly has an understanding of our military and what this great country owes to all our veterans. I suspect she may be on the right track to a career in journalism.

When Kaitlyn was little, Sheila and I took her over to our neighbor's dairy farm and I asked them if we could take Kaitlyn over to see the newly born calves. They said "yes" and Kaitlyn had a blast petting all the calves. When we got home, she told her grammy that she had to wash her hands because they were all yucky from the calves licking them. Another time we were in the car, passing a field full of cows, so I stopped for Kaitlyn to get a good look. She said, "look grammy, the cows are eatin' and poopin'."

When the kids sleep over it has become a tradition that Kaitlyn make pancakes in the morning for all of us. It all started a few years ago when she asked Sheila if she could help her make the pancakes. Some mornings I would have to leave for work before the kids woke up so Kaitlyn would make my pancakes and put them in the refrigerator for me to have when I got home from work.

Just recently, Sheila had to leave early for work so Kaitlyn was on her own for the first time. I asked Sheila if she could make the pancakes on her own and Sheila said she could, that I would just have to keep an eye on her. Kaitlyn said we had to call Grammy to find out how high the stove needed to be. We have a long griddle that covers two burners and Sheila told me the numbers to set them at. Well, I went a little higher than she said and the pancakes started to burn. Later in the day, Sheila was on the phone with Kaitlyn and I yelled out, "Kaitlyn burned the pancakes Grammy." Kaitlyn yelled back, "Pappy had the burners too high." Oh, I forgot to mention, Kaitlyn wants to open her own house of pancakes.

On the day we found out A.J. had died, Tyna, Rick and the kids came over to the house. I remember being in a state of deep depression, but when Kaitlyn came over and gave me a kiss, and I held her in my arms, the bad feelings washed away, and I was so happy she was there for me. She asked me, "pappy, who's going to protect us from the bad guys now?" I told her that A.J. would still be watching over us.

A few days later, some soldiers who were friends of A.J. came to the house and I mentioned to them about the question Kaitlyn asked me. They went over to her and told her that they would help protect her now, and she shouldn't worry. She smiled and told them, "thank you." I know that made her feel better, and the rest of us were grateful for the soldier's gesture.

FRIENDS

Chapter 13

Approximately six months after A.J. died, there was another casualty in our area: Sgt. Matthew J. Sandri of Shamokin, Pa. Matt was a combat medic with Charlie Company, 82nd Forward Support Battalion, 3rd Brigade Combat Team of the 82nd Airborne Division. He died as a result of injuries sustained in a rocket attack where he worked at Forward Operating Base, Sainte Mere Eglise, near Fallujah, Iraq. The attack also killed Lt. Colonel Mark Taylor, a physician with the 82nd, and wounded five soldiers and one sailor. Matt was killed in action on March 20, 2004. In December of 2008, a state of the art medical training facility was dedicated at Ft. Bragg, North Carolina, named the Taylor - Sandri Medical Training Center. It allows 5,000 troops per year, the virtual experience of treating simulated combat wounds, using electronic monitors and multiple cameras. The center better prepares combat medics going into harm's way, better than ever before. I can only imagine the number of lives that will be saved on the battlefield because of this new facility.

I had planned a trip to my brother's house in North Carolina around that time and had every intention of attending this paratrooper's funeral. I figured by the time I returned from my trip, preparations would be in order for Matt's burial. When A.J. died his body was not returned to us for weeks so I thought the same would hold true for the Sandri family. When I came back from North Carolina I learned that the funeral was over and I was deeply saddened. I called the Sandris and introduced myself and apologized for missing Matt's funeral. Bob Sandri, Matt's father, and I spoke at great length and decided we needed to get together. The only problem was that every time we would try to arrange a meeting, it would fall through for one reason or another. Well, we finally did get to meet and Sheila and I have become the best of friends with this warm, wonderful family of Matt's. Bob and I are both members of the Central Pa. Chapter of the 82nd Airborne Association, and the meetings are on the first Sunday of the month. After the meetings Bob and I head down the street to a Thai Restaurant and have a feast. We usually get together with the Sandris over Memorial Day and Veteran's Day in Washington, D.C. and attend activities with the 82nd Abn. Association.

Last April, our families were invited to Washington to meet the Ambassador of Iraq, Samir S. Sumaida'ie. There was a memorial service in Arlington National Cemetery in remembrance of Iraq Liberation Day. Bob called me and said his family couldn't make it and would I like to go with him. I told Sheila and she said she would not be able to get off work so I should go with Bob. So we went to the ceremony and it was quite impressive. Afterward, we were all invited to dinner at the Ft. Myer Officer's Club. We were seated at tables that had Iraqi Embassy workers seated at them and it made for interesting conversation. Bob and I had two very nice young ladies seated next to us and they told us they were from Baghdad and would be working at the embassy for a year and then return to Iraq. The Iraqi's could not thank us enough for our son's sacrifice for their people. After dinner, the ambassador stood up to speak, and he told us he feels what we are going through because he had lost three brothers in the war. He spoke quite well and we listened intently to what this warmhearted man had to say. Then, an Iraqi General stood up and spoke some words of thanks on behalf of his country. We were then told that as a soldier's name was announced, one family member was to come forward to accept a memento. The Iraqi Ambassador shook our hands and made the presentation to each family.

When I opened the box, inside there was a clear glass cube approximately three by five inches and as I looked at it, inside was the image of an Assyrian Winged Bull, and an inscription:

"On behalf of the Government and People of Iraq, I have the great honor and distinct privilege to present this token of DEEP GRATITUDE for your hero's sacrifice and your personal loss.
-Samir S. Sumaida'ie."

After the presentations ended I went over to have a photo taken with the Ambassador and I thanked him and reached into my pocket and pulled out a cigar. I said to him, "you have given me a gift, now I have one for you." He smiled and thanked me.

As Bob and I milled around we ran into General Richard Rowe, the man who oversaw A.J.'s funeral in Arlington. It just so happens that he is the Commanding General of the Military District of Washington. We met the general's wife and had a very nice conversation. We also met a general from the British Defense Staff of Washington, D.C. It was a wonderful event and Bob and I were so glad we attended.

The next day Bob and I were on our way to see the National Cathedral and as we headed up Embassy Row we noticed the Iraqi Embassy. We looked at one another and Bob said, "what the hell, the girls gave us their business cards." I replied, "yeah, let's try it, I've never been in an embassy before." So we parked the car and went up to the front door and rang the doorbell. We were immediately let in an approached a man sitting at a reception desk and explained that we had been with the ambassador the night before. We showed him the cards the girls gave us and he ushered us into an anteroom. He said to make ourselves comfortable and he would see if they were available. A short time later, one of the young ladies came into the room and we shook hands. We had a nice conversation and had our pictures taken with her in front of the Iraqi flag.

We then said goodbye and went to see the cathedral and then stopped by a Thai restaurant to fill up before heading home. It was a great trip, Bob is a good traveling companion and tour guide, he used to work in Washington. On another trip, this time with the Sandri family, which included Bob's wife Annette, son Blake, and daughter Lydia, (their oldest daughter, Julie, could not attend), our destination was once again our nation's capitol. It was Veteran's day weekend of 2008. We met the Sandri's at Mt. Vernon and did a tour which was very informative. This stop was at the request of Lydia. While we were there we ran into Ruth Stonesifer, who also lost her son in a helicopter crash in the mountains of Pakistan en route to Afghanistan. Kristofor was an Army Ranger involved in Operation Rhino on October 19, 2001. Ruth is the President of the Pennsylvania Gold Star Mothers, and was instrumental in the passage of House Bill 2498, signed by Governor Ed Rendell on October 4, 2006. This bill made it possible for all Pennsylvania Gold Star Families to obtain special license plates, designating them as Gold Star Families who had lost a loved one in the Global War on Terror.

The next morning we went for a tour of the Pentagon, which Bob arranged through an airman who works there, and is a friend of their family. The building is huge and we did an awful lot of walking. Our guide took us to where American Airlines Flight 77 crashed into the Pentagon. There is a large window and as you look out, he tells you exactly where the plane made its approach, and outside is a memorial garden to all the people who lost their lives. There is a room with large books that have all the names of those people, including their photo, and a short story about them and why they were on Flight 77 that day. It is truly a moving experience and something I felt honored to see.

After that, we were informed that the Sandris had to leave to head for New York City. It seems daughter Lydia wrote President Bush a letter telling him how disappointed she was that she didn't get to meet him when he visited Ft. Bragg back in June of 2005. Well, the Sandri family was invited to meet President Bush during the rededication ceremony aboard the USS Intrepid.

They left and we did the town on our own. After a final visit to Arlington later in the day to visit A.J.'s gravesite, we headed north. On the way home we called the Sandris and Lydia got on the phone, all excited, telling us they met with President Bush, received his presidential coin, and also got an invitation to visit him in the oval office. This transpired because in Lydia's letter, she said she always wanted to see the Resolute Desk, from the movie National Treasure. They had quite a trip, and so did we.

Another family we have become good friends with is the Barbieri family. Sheila and I met Tom and Carol Barbieri a few years ago during Veterans Day in Washington. We were part of the 82nd Airborne Association entourage and happened to be in the dining area of the hotel when Tom and Carol were introduced to us. Their son T.J. had also been a member of the 82nd Airborne Division. Specialist T.J. Barbieri was assigned to the 1/325th Parachute Infantry Regiment. His patrol encountered enemy forces and began taking small arms fire south of Baghdad. Barbieri assaulted heavily armed enemy combatants who were occupying a strong ambush position with dominating fields of fire. Utilizing his SAW (squad automatic weapon), he conducted a daring assault on the flank of the enemy force, exposing himself in full view of the enemy, in order to bring his weapon to bear and prevent enemy fire on his platoon sergeant and the rest of his platoon located in the ambush kill zone. T.J. killed one enemy combatant and made possible the elimination of the second, but only at the cost of his own life.

Spc. Barbieri was awarded the Silver Star, Bronze Star, and Purple Heart. He is buried near my son in Section 60, Arlington National Cemetery.

Tom and Carol Barbieri live 15 minutes from Arlington and they always make it a point to put flowers on A.J.'s gravesite whenever they visit. Not only that, Tom makes it a point to take a picture with his cell phone and send it to mine. T.J. was known for his great sense of humor, and just recently, Tom was telling me a story about his son. T.J.'s unit was trying to come up with a catchy nickname, so they were sitting around a table and each one got his turn to come up with a name. The usual stuff went around the table such as "The Destroyers" or "Death Dealers" and so on. When T.J.'s turn came, he said, "The Sweatpants Boners." He said it was a name that would make others take notice. When you think about it, he was absolutely right.

Sheila and I have been blessed to have such great friends through all of this, and we keep meeting more. We are part of an exclusive club, one that no one would ever want to join. But being in it has given us the opportunity to meet many, many new acquaintances.

Coincidentally, my daughter Elizabeth is going to have another baby. They already know it will be a boy, and the name that she and Shack have chosen is Tyler Joseph. Break that down and it becomes T.J. Things that make you go "humm."

BACK TO BRAGG

Chapter 14

I was reading an article someone sent me about an artist by the name of Michael Reagan, an internationally recognized artist, who did portraits for families who had lost a loved one in Iraq and Afghanistan. As a portrait artist for over thirty years, Reagan has drawn approximately ten thousand portraits, including over fifteen hundred of celebrities, professional athletes, U.S. Presidents, and other heads of state. He discovered his talent as a youth when he was looking for a distraction while recovering from a football injury. As a combat Marine in Vietnam, Reagan often drew portraits of other Marines. "I drew portraits of lots of Marines whose pictures came back but they didn't." Says Reagan. "It is only through the grace of God that I have come back alive. Given a second chance on life, I am making the most of it, including sharing my talent with others." This remarkable man did a portrait of our son A.J. and as I look at his likeness, I swear I am gazing right into my son's eyes. It is so life like, and words alone could never express my gratitude for the wonderful gift Michael

Reagan has given us. He is more than an artist, he is one of God's special creatures. Thank you Michael.

One day in June of 2005, I was sitting at my computer and the phone rang. I answered it and from the other end a man's voice asked for Mr. Baddick. I said I was Mr. Baddick and he introduced himself as a Lieutenant from Ft.Bragg. He said, "would you be interested in meeting the president?" I asked, "the president of what?" The lieutenant replied, "the President of the United States, George W. Bush." I hesitated a moment and came back with, "You gotta be shittin' me." He said this was the real deal and that the President was coming to Ft. Bragg and wished to meet with families that had lost a trooper from the 82nd. How could I refuse to meet A.J.'s Commander in Chief? I told the lieutenant "yes." He said he would take care of the details and asked me to call back with family members that would be attending. Sheila and I dropped everything and started to make arrangements to travel down to Ft. Bragg.

I received a phone call from SSG. Alan Meador, who was in A.J.'s unit, and he explained that he would be our escort while we were at Ft. Bragg. He gave me a number to call when we arrived and he came to our motel to meet with us. After introductions Alan explained that he first met A.J. in 2003, just before they deployed to Iraq. He told us they were in different squads but had rooms next to each other.

Alan explained that on the night A.J. died, he was on a patrol and word came in to get over to the incident area ASAP. He was shocked to hear what had happened and who was missing. They began assisting in searching both sides of the canal. He said an Air Force search and rescue team was brought in and divers entered the water. Alan was sad to hear that in the morning A.J.'s body was recovered. He attended A.J.'s memorial service and remembered how A.J. enjoyed training other soldiers and how he took good care of his people. He said A.J. loved the Army.

Alan said he would return in the morning to pick us up. The following morning Alan arrived and had another trooper with him by the name of Ben Dellinger. They were both fine examples of 82nd Airborne paratroopers. Alan explained that we had to park our car somewhere near the base and go in his vehicle. Ben rode with me, and on the way I asked Ben to tell me something about A.J. He asked me, "what?" I said, "tell me anything you remember." Ben told me, "well, when A.J. grabbed the soldier that was going under and swam him over to the edge of the canal, he handed the soldier off to us and he said, "man, I got some of that shitty canal water in my mouth and it ruined my chew." Then Ben made a motion with his finger like he was removing the chew from his mouth." I said, "thanks Ben, that sounds just like my son, those are the things you don't hear on an official Army report." I told him, "aside from meeting the President, that is the highlight of my trip, thank you."

We were to learn later on that Ben deployed once again to Iraq and was involved in an IED explosion near Baghdad. His convoy was hit but no one was injured. As they were searching on foot for secondary devices, Ben practically stepped on one. The explosion started low and took off the lower part of his left leg. His other ankle and a shoulder were broken. Ben would spend a lot of time at Walter Reed Medical Center recovering and learning to walk again with his new prosthetic leg, so hi tech that it exceeded his expectations. The Purple Heart recipient joined the Army in response to the September 11 attacks. Ben plans on a career with the DEA in the near future. My wife and I wish him all the best in his career.

When we entered Ft. Bragg, Alan told us A.J.'s Sergeant Major wanted to meet with us so we headed over to the 504th area. Alan took us into headquarters and asked us to wait in the lobby until he let them know we were there. On the wall were pictures of paratroopers from the unit that had been lost in action, and one of them was A.J. We were ushered into Sergeant Major Love's office and we talked about A.J. for awhile and I asked the Sergeant Major if he was aware that I was a former member of the 504th. He said "no" and asked me what battalion I was in. Well, there are three battalions, the 1st which is known as the Red Devils, 2nd is the White Devils, and 3rd is the Blue Devils. The Sergeant Major is a black man and I answered him with, "I was in the 2nd battalion." His reply was, "oh, you were a White Devil." I pointed my finger at him and came back with, "Who you callin' a White Devil?" Well, I'll tell you what, we had a good laugh over that one. Sergeant Major Love was the genuine article and it was a real pleasure meeting him. I'm glad my son had the opportunity to serve under such a good man.

After that we were driven over to where we would meet with President Bush. We were taken into a building that was rather large with a stage in the front. Many families were gathered inside, approximately thirty or more. It was my belief that the President would enter the building, walk around, shake hands, and tell the families how sorry he was, but was I in for a surprise. A man made an announcement that families would be put into their own individual rooms. It would be done alphabetically and those with small children would be first. We met both criteria, as our last name started with B, and we had our granddaughter, Andi Rose with us. We were in a room about ten minutes when the door opened and President Bush walked in. As we stared like a bunch of goofs, he said, "It's really me." Sheila was first in the reception line so he went to her and she said, "Mr. President." With that, he placed his arm around her and said, "no, no, it's George W." Then he gave her a kiss on the cheek and they talked a bit. Then he came to me, we shook hands and I said, "Sir, even though we've lost our son, we are behind you one hundred percent. Don't lose sight of what you've started and don't drop the ball or our son's life and the lives of all the other soldiers will be for nothing." He looked me square in the eye and said for us to listen to his speech tonight from Ft. Bragg and his message would be loud and clear. He placed his presidential coin in our hands and went around the room talking to A.J.'s mom, her husband Jack, my daughter Elizabeth, and her husband Shack. He asked if we would like pictures and we all said yes. There was photographer from the White House there and also two Secret Service Agents. President Bush took Andi Rose in his arms and cameras started snapping. I can see Andi Rose in the future at school on show and tell day, with her 8X10 glossy showing President George W. Bush holding her in his arms. Before he left he offered his condolences for our loss and Sheila's eyes started to well up. Once again, George W. Bush came over, tears in his eyes, put his arm around her and said, "let's cry together," and they did. Sheila received another kiss on the cheek and the President left. I know there are many people who did not care for this president but he is the real article. He put us at ease as soon as he came in the room. He spent about ten minutes with us and then had to do the same with all the other families, which I'm sure was not easy. One thing I will say about George W. Bush: like him or not, he kept the citizens of our great country safe from terrorist attacks during his entire time in office, and that is the President's number one priority. I'd say, "Mission Accomplished."

The following day, we were escorted on post for a tour of A.J.'s former unit, where they had a small ceremony in his honor, and to show us a beautiful headstone, in his memory, that they had placed right outside the entrance to the barracks of A. Co. / 1st Battalion / 504th Infantry. We had the opportunity to meet some of the soldiers A.J. served with, and they told us that they collected money from the unit to have a memorial made, and contracted a guy to make it. When they went to pick it up, they said it looked like some five year old made it and they told him to keep it. They then collected more money and had another one made that now holds a place of honor where all troopers entering A Company's barracks can see it. It is absolutely beautiful and greatly appreciated by our family. We were then invited to the chow hall for a bite to eat, and I must say, Army chow has come a long way from the time I was there. The food was quite good, but then, an army does move on its stomach. We also made a visit to the Main PX and bought a few items.

The following day we said our goodbyes to Alan and Ben, thanking them for the time they spent with us, and wishing them all the best. We headed north with a stop at Arlington National Cemetery on the way home.

We were once again invited to Ft. Bragg for the Memorial Day Weekend of 2008. This time there was to be a dedication ceremony of the Global War on Terrorism Memorial. We decided we would really like to attend this and also take in the All American Week activities that take place each year at this time. During AA Week there are competitions between the units, special tours, a golf tournament, band concert, open PX, breakfast and lunch with the paratroopers, and get togethers at the Fayetteville, 82nd Association Clubhouse. There is a Division Review at the parade grounds and a Joint Training Exercise out at Sicily drop zone. It starts with a combat parachute jump and a demonstration of the awesome ability of the 82nd paratroopers to take and hold an enemy position with assistance from the 82nd's Aviation Brigade, flying Apache helicopters. In addition to that, there are static displays set up so all visitors may get an up close look at all the hardware employed by the 82nd Airborne Division.

A few days before we left, we were contacted by SSG. Zack Kraphl, a trooper in 1/504th, and he informed us he would be acting as our escort this trip. He gave us his phone number and told us to call him when we arrived. The first order of business was a rather large picnic out at McKellar's Lodge, hosted by the 82nd Association. We called Zack and told him we'd be out at the picnic and he should join us. We were having a good time with some friends and finally Zack showed up and we introduced him around and had some pleasant conversation. Later on he told us he had to get home to take care of his young son, so he told us he's be by early in the morning to pick us up.

The next day Zack took us into Ft. Bragg and we headed over to Pike Field for the Division Review. There was a rumor flying around that President Bush was going to make an appearance and just before the ceremonies were about to begin, there was an announcement that the President had arrived and was on his way in. We looked toward the entrance and guards had moved the people back and cordoned off a walkway about thirty feet wide. We could see men in black suits and Sheila decided she was going to take a picture of Mr. Bush. She told me to help her up on her chair and I asked her, "Sheila, you have an eight by ten photo of us with President Bush, isn't that good enough?" She immediately responded with, "no."

Anyway, in walked the President and he headed over to the grandstand to say some words. He spoke about how proud he was to be visiting Ft. Bragg once more, but said he wouldn't be making any jumps. He remarked that his father would remain the only parachuting president in the family.

Now, we have seen Division Reviews before and normally the highest ranking person is driven by the division, for review, in a vehicle. This Commander in Chief was having none of that, he walked out to the field and walked past the ranks of the entire division and then walked back. I was impressed and so were many others. After the Division Review, Zack told us we were to get over to the 82nd Museum as soon as possible for the Memorial Ceremony and Dedication of the Global War on Terrorism Memorial.

When we arrived there was supposed to be assigned seating for all the Gold Star families but they had trouble finding our seats. I went over to a sergeant and asked where we could sit. He pointed to some seats with no names on them and we sat. A short time later, another sergeant came over and asked us to move, he needed our seats. He showed us another section of seats and said we could sit there, and we did. Finally, the first sergeant who moved us came over and asked us to follow him. He seated us in the second row, and by now we were hoping this was final. Well, unbeknownst to us, Zack was in the rear watching us play musical chairs and decided to get involved. He explained to the sergeant that we were Gold Star parents and were being treated unfairly and if he didn't want Zack to take the matter up with someone of authority, he'd better find us good seats. That's how we ended up with top notch seats.

As we're sitting there, we notice a Secret Service agent come over to the only empty seat just in front of us and to our left, and he places a bottle of water on a presidential napkin, on the ground. Sheila looks at me and asks me what that's for. Now, I'm thinking the Secret Service agent is going to sit there but I'm telling Sheila, "George W. is probably going to sit there." About five minutes later, out of the blue, the President comes over and plops his butt in the empty chair. We see him put his arm around the woman next to him who has lost her husband and he consoles her as they talk a bit. He then turns to the family on the other side of him and talks to them for awhile.

As he turns around to his right I hold up the presidential coin he gave me back in 2005 and he looks at it, then us, and says, "nice to see you folks again." "Nice to see you too Mr. President," we replied.

The memorial and dedication service was very moving. The GWOT Memorial has the names of all the 82nd paratroopers who gave their lives, engraved on it. When all the guest speakers were finished, each Gold Star family member had a yellow rose, and we were asked to go up and lay our roses at the foot of the monument. Mr. Bush stood up and greeted each family member with a handshake or hug.

There was a mother in attendance, Francie Dembowski, whose son, PFC Robert H. Dembowski, was killed on 24 May, 2007 in Iraq. Robert was in A.J.'s unit, 1/504th and he was also from Pennsylvania. He died of wounds he received when his unit came under attack near Baghdad, Iraq. Dembo, as his friends called him, received the Bronze Star and Purple Heart. His friends would say he had a way of brightening even the darkest days during their deployment. His mother wrote this beautiful poem:

"If You Saw The Pile Of Roses

If you saw the pile of roses,
Gently laid upon the ground
By the families for the heroes
Soldiers who laid their own lives down

To try to make things better
In this world before they'd go
If you saw the pile of roses
And the tears that over-flowed.

There were families of the fallen
They were looking everywhere
For the face of that one soldier
They knew was no longer there.
There were wounded, crippled soldiers
Mangled legs, and missing arms
Head all scarred from surgeries
And eyes that stared afar.

Other heroes, stood encircling
Soldiers supporting those within
Standing tall and proud and strong
Suffering silently from within.

These soldiers felt such sadness
They'd lost friends and felt such grief.
They carried wounded warriors.
They love their country.
They long for peace.

They are heroes beyond measure
So young, brave, kind, and strong
They'll grow to be our veterans
With God's grace, before too long.

So please honor all our heroes,

Fallen, wounded, young and old
All those who guard our country
Our cities and our homes.

Just thank them for their service
And the sacrifices made
If you saw the pile of roses...
You'd know...

It's a difficult price to pay."

The following day Zack came to take us to the Joint Readiness Training Exercise out at Sicily drop zone. On the way out to the drop zone, Zack told us how he remembered playing cards with A.J. They would play Texas Hold 'Em and Zack said A.J. was really good, and that he lost quite a bit of money to him. I told Zack that was one thing he didn't learn that from me.

It was a nice day and the 82nd put on a hell of a show. It was quite a sight watching all of the paratroopers exit the aircraft and float to earth. It sure brought back memories for me. I remembered watching A.J.'s contribution to the exercise only a few short years earlier, how he jumped in and secured the mock airfield with his unit, and then the grueling walk in to where we were. The first thing out of his mouth was, "I need a Gatorade."

As we watched the exercise and the Apache helicopters standing off a distance for support, Zack began to tell us about the time he had need of their assistance. His unit was engaged in a fire fight with the enemy and he decided to call in an Apache to assist them. The pilot asked

Zack to fire tracers at the enemy building and he began firing. The pilot told him to stop, he could not see the tracers. The pilot brought the chopper down so low, Zack could touch one of the skids. The pilot told Zack to fire again, and as he did, the pilot said, "okay, I got it now." Zack told us the Apache let loose on the building and the enemy took off running like rats off of a sinking ship. He said they had twenty two confirmed kills that day.

In October of 2003, Zack would receive the Purple Heart Award. His unit was traveling outside of the Abu Ghraib Prison when two 155mm rounds buried in the road exploded. He said the situation was more calm and surreal than anything. He says, "I simply remember waking up shortly after we had been engulfed by a large ball of fire. I couldn't hear anything else going on around me, and I was bleeding from the ears and nose, among some other places. There was a little piece of shrapnel that had gone through the gun truck and was sticking into my calf, part way in. Thank God though, because it was the size of a Dorito chip."

Zack's second Purple Heart Award would come during the surge of 2007. "A friend and I were going to get haircuts on the FOB (Forward Operating Base), and we started to argue which would be the fastest way to get there. Ultimately, I decided to listen to him, and we took a short cut through the motor pool. Suddenly, we heard a shallow thud, and questioned what had made the sound. We both determined that it sounded like outgoing more than anything. Well, we were wrong. The next 60mm mortar round hit no more than ten feet away, knocking us both to the ground. We rushed into a building, and Sgt

Szalai told me I was bleeding from the face. I didn't really know it, until he gave me a 'paper towel' to put on my face. When I put the towel on my face, I got the sensation that my face was on fire. It felt as if there was a lighter under my chin. I pulled back the paper towel, smelled it, and sure enough, it wasn't a paper towel. He had given me a fabric softener sheet, and it didn't stop the bleeding. When the attack was over, I bitched and moaned all the way over to the AID Station. I was so pissed off, I mean, really, what are the odds, what are the fucking odds? I know now though, a lot better than I thought."

After the exercise was over, we headed back to attend a picnic at the 82nd Airborne Association Fayetteville Chapter's Clubhouse. The food was delicious and we had many laughs that day.

We got ready to head north the next day. Our next stop was to be Washington, D.C., to visit A.J's gravesite. Before we left, Zack came over and said he had a gift for us. It was a framed photo of him in full battle gear over in the desert. We thanked him, and with a tear in our eyes we said goodbye. That picture sits in our living room still. Thank you Zack Kraphl, for helping to make our trip a memorable one. You are a real American Soldier, and a credit to the 82nd Airborne Division and the United States of America.

We had the pleasure of spending some time with Zack, his lovely wife Mandy, and their two sons, Killian and Cavin. We were back at Ft. Bragg for a Memorial Ceremony at the GWOT memorial. Zack was once again our escort. SSG. Zack Kraphl is currently on his 6th combat tour. When I asked him his thoughts about deploying to

Iraq once again, he replied, "I wish I were going to Afghanistan, that is where all the action is now, Iraq will be boring."

REMEMBERING A.J.

Chapter 15

As time went by I found out about different websites and forums that dealt with soldiers who had died in the Global War on Terror. It really amazed me that there are so many nice people out there with kind words to say about my son. I would like to share some of their comments:

"Sgt. Baddick, I think you were the best RTO in division, yet you wanted to go to the Red Devils to make your dad proud. I talked to the Sergeant Major to let you go to the Red Devils and you spoke to 1st Sergeant Hacker and he took you in. You did what you had been wanting to do since the war started. I didn't want you to go, but I had to help you get there. I still dream of you and I dream of swimming after you and I am always out of reach. I love you Baddick, you are a great soldier!!!"
-WM of Ft. Bragg

"Baddick… my goofy friend. It has been six years since you made me smile. I knew you would be a good friend. You made me realize how precious life is…….I will never forget you."

-Frances of Killeen, Texas

"Baddick, I can remember your airborne tattoo before you ever went to airborne school. You were one of a kind. You will not be forgotten. Kilo 1st 75th. - To the Baddick family, I served with Baddick at Ft. Hood and cried the day I found out he had past. I would like to let you know that I operate a non-profit that helps soldiers and have a store with adorning boots, rifle, and helmet ……in memory of Sgt. Andrew Baddick. He will not be forgotten."

-Sgt. Patrick Sowers of Dallas, Texas

"Wow, A.J... it has been almost 5 years, and I still think of you often. I was searching on the internet for your name and saw a picture of your mom and sister and family at your burial at Arlington. As I look at your mother, my heart breaks. Especially now that I am a mother of two. Knowing who you were and everything you have done, not only for our country, but the people who you loved and cared for the most. I only wish that I could see you one more time to let you know how proud of you I am. I miss you A.J. I love you."

-Autum Curran of Yokota AB, Japan

"To the family of Sgt. Andrew Joseph Baddick: Andrew gave the ultimate sacrifice and will be held in the hearts of Americans forever. I cannot, and will not let our fallen heroes be forgotten. My deepest sympathy to you. 'Some Gave All.' Don't let the memory of them drift away."
-Peggy Childers of Carson City, Nevada

"A.J. - I first read your name over four years ago, the day that I found out that one of my best friends was not coming home again, Sgt. Potter, the one you tried to save, but couldn't. Three weeks ago, I went out on a blind date with a guy that was in the 82nd - so naturally I started talking Army, and Darrin came up, and then so did you. Turns out that each of you guys were one of our closest friends. Talk about a WOW experience!!!!!! We both got goose bumps, teared up, and were in complete shock and awe when we realized that our stories of how our friends died over there were meshed together. You guys have made the ultimate sacrifice for all of us over here, and there are really no words that can express the appreciation, gratitude, and pride that I have for Ya'll. A.J., I never met you, but from what Curtis has told me about you, and just the fact that you tried to save my best friend - I know that you were a man of honor and served our country well, and your family can be proud of you! Thank You!!! I know you are missed."
-Liberty Burke of Sarasota, Florida, USA

"After all this time I can still picture Andrew's face when he first arrived in my platoon in 2-8 Infantry. I will never forget my first new private! It was an honor!"
-Stefan of Ft. Chaffee, AR

"I was there when A.J. jumped into the canal. He went in, in a flash, to save those men. He was able to get one to the side of the canal where we were able to get him out. When someone said, the other guy, whom I afterward found out to be Sgt. Potter, got swept under the bridge, he said 'I got him' and went under. Although he and I didn't always see eye to eye, my respect for him multiplied by an infinite value that night. He jumped in the current to save a man who he didn't know in any way other than he be a brother in need of help."
-Robert Latta, A.Co. 1-504th PIR

"Andrew, I would like to say thank you for your service and sacrifice for our Country - not just in Iraq, but also for your service in Afghanistan as well. And to your family and loved ones, I wish to extend my deepest sympathy. You are the epitome of what an Army NCO is supposed to be - you didn't hesitate to try to save the life of a fellow soldier who you didn't even know - that says everything about the kind of man you are."
-Airborne All The Way

"To the family of Joseph Baddick: Words cannot express the way I feel about Andrew. As I read over the messages that people have left, I feel a connection between Andrew and Darrin. Andrew lost his life trying to save my stepbrother, and Darrin died while looking over his fellow soldiers. Sgt. Baddick and Sgt. Potter are the reasons we are free today, and we couldn't be more proud of them." WE WILL NOT FORGET! All Gave Some… These Heroes Gave All.

-Jon Campbell of Louisville, Kentucky, Land of the Free, and Home of the Brave.

"Three years to the date, I have not forgotten. As I prepare for my third trip over to that hell hole I am looking for redemption and redemption will be served. I have not forgotten you as a friend, classmate, and hero. We had many good times together and I will never forget them. See you in the next life. God Speed."

-SSGT. TJ Garritano, 111th FW-A10 Warthogs

"A.J., I haven't left a message before because I didn't know you like most of the others knew you. However, you were still a friend to me. We were stationed together in Afghanistan. I would often relieve you from duty and vise versa. We would converse about our hardships, however, you always had a positive outlook. I'll never forget the time that……when we came home from Afghanistan and you ran into my father on the

beach in Wrightsville. He was wearing an 82nd shirt.....you asked him about me.....of all the people in that damn division you ran into my father. It had to be the one time, when asked if you know a soldier, that it turned out he and you did. That was my last memory of you. You were and are still a hero. May your friends and family be proud."
-FMR Sgt. Burton, Derick S. of Moline, Illinois.

"Well, I just want to say that every time I feel sorry for myself I look at that metal around my wrist that has Sgt. Andrew J. Baddick's name on it and think to myself how hard it was for him and his family. The will to never give up is what he has left for me. Thank you."
-PFC Joseph Padilla stationed in Seoul / Yongson Garrison / Republic of Korea. Ft. Bragg 2006

"I met A.J. while at jump school. We made quick friends and hung out at airborne school. The last time I saw him was when I dropped him off at the airport, after training was complete, so he could fly home to see his family. I was deeply saddened to read in the paper, later that year, of his loss. I remember the last day I saw him, he was very excited to be a paratrooper, like his father. I am proud to have known A.J., he is a hero. God Bless A.J. and the Baddick family."
-SFC Dan, 19th Special Forces Group, Deployed.

"A.J., I miss you my little brother. I'm so proud that you took my advice and finished school and joined the military. You made yourself a true man and a hero. Wish I could have been with you. You will always be in my heart and we will meet again. From your Big Brother Bob. I love you bro!"
-MA3 USN Robert Transue of Stroudsburg

"I referred to A.J. as 'Bad-Baddick.' He was one of the best and could be counted on to get the job done. He was my driver in Afghanistan while we worked with the 82nd's G-3. He volunteered for line duty and went to the 504th. I attended his funeral at Arlington and had the honor of meeting his family and especially his father. We live in freedom because of men like Andrew Joseph Baddick. Gone but Not Forgotten. Rest in Peace Brother."
-Big Jim Miller CSM, USA, Ret. of Jacksonville, N.C.

"I had the honor to serve with Andrew Baddick when we were both serving in the 82nd Airborne Division. Sgt. Baddick was an outstanding paratrooper who was proud to serve his country. He was especially proud to serve in the same unit that his father had served in. Andrew always carried a picture of his father with him and was quick to show it off. The morning after his death, we were all saddened but not surprised at the circumstances. I attended his memorial service

along with the Commanding General of the 82nd and was proud to have known him."
-Michael Duke, Sergeant Major (Ret) of Raeford, N.C.

"(Private First Class), that was your rank when we last parted ways in Texas. Sergeant Baddick, do you remember me? I was your Company Commander then and your soul-mate now. No one feels the sting of your passing more than I. I think of you every single day. Baddick, you were not happy being an average Joe. No sir, you wanted to jump out of airplanes. You wanted to be Hooah. I re-enlisted you, and sent you to airborne school, en route to the 82nd Airborne Division. I am so proud of you. You made this world a better place, thanks. Andrew my friend, you are the best of the best."
-Major Charles E. Greene of Anchorage, Alaska

"I was out on patrol the night this hero tried to save my friend. I personally never got the honor of meeting Andrew but know that one day we will meet and I will thank him for being the soldier that all would be proud to serve with. Last year, I had taken a trip out to California to visit a friend. Out on one of the beaches they had a cross for every soldier killed since the war began. I asked where I could find Darrin Potter and Andrew Baddick, they said there was no telling. You see, they would put these crosses out every single Sunday, so Americans would not forget, but they placed them

in and out of the sand in no particular order due to the large numbers. So I began searching....45 minutes later, there he was, 'Sgt. Darrin K. Potter' my friend forever. I sat there and talked to him for what seemed an eternity and then got up and started looking for Andrew and to my amazement, out of these hundreds upon hundreds of soldiers that had died fighting for freedom and for each other, there he was.....right next to Darrin. How had I not noticed before, how had I not seen? So there I fell to my knees at the wonders of God.....they had stuck together, Andrew went in for him and found him. To the parents of the bravest soldier I never met , I pray for your strength everyday. May you find peace."
-Sgt. Schelee K. Reece of Louisvlle, KY, 223rd Military Police Company

"To the family and friends of Sgt. Baddick. I was reminded of Sgt. Baddick as I was reading through some letters which my fiance sent me from Iraq. He was in HQ 1/504, and he wrote me about Sgt. Baddick's selfless, heroic act to try and save Sgt. Potter. I am truly sorry for your loss. I have come to know that loss personally, as my fiance, Cpt. Ernesto Blanco, was killed three months later. May the Lord bless you and help you make it through."
-Michelle Blanco of Texas

"I served alongside Andrew's unit at Abu Ghraib, Iraq. I will never forget the night he died trying to

save a National Guard MP, Sgt. Darrin Potter, from drowning. I never met Andrew personally, but it's soldiers like him that make me proud to have served in such a horrible place. God Bless your family Andrew!"
-George Sakellakis of Cleveland, Ohio

"To the family of Sgt. Andrew Joseph Baddick. I didn't know your son, but I feel proud to wear a uniform because of men like him. He made the ultimate sacrifice to save someone else and that's a prime example of what soldiering is all about. Every morning service men and women salute our flag in remembrance of the soldiers that died for it. I'll think of Andrew Joseph Baddick because his selfless service has truly defined Army values for me. You should all be proud of your soldier. My prayers go to you."
-SSG. Ortiz of South Korea

"This old paratrooper will never forget the brotherhood of the greatest division in the world. Although I never ran across Baddick, my heart still hurts for my brother. May you rest in peace."
-Anthony of Denver, CO

"This just makes me want to go to war and help out our fellow Americans, and I am highly thinking of doing it. I came across this and my name is Andrew Joseph Thomas, alas, my family calls me A.J. I am thinking of becoming a paratrooper too.

Just thought that was interesting and I'm sorry for ya'lls loss. I will remember this great soldier and man."
-Andrew Thomas of Denton, Texas USA

"I actually recognized Sgt. Baddick after seeing his photo. It finally dawned on me that we crossed paths at Ft. Bragg, and I actually had the honor, the privilege, of having a brief conversation with an American Hero."
-Eric S. Ex 325th AIR, 2/82nd of Elk Grove, CA.

"I have to say, I never knew Andrew, but he seems quite amazing. He is definitely a hero. I am so proud and greatly honored to have people like him in our military. I am so sorry for your loss, and I am sorry that this great man had to leave us so soon. I will tell all my friends about Andrew's great heroism so we never forget the sacrifices that he and all of the soldiers in the U.S. Military made for all of us… Take Care."
-Jessica of Cincinnati, OH

"A.J. was my cousin. I would like to thank him for the great sacrifice he has made for this country's freedom. A.J. is definitely MY HERO."
-Karlee Stempel of White Haven, Pa. USA

"Sgt. Baddick, goodbye soldier and thank you. You are my hero."
-Bill of Houston, Texas

"What a true American Hero! He was not only there to protect our lives and willing to give his for our freedom, but he also gave his life to try and save another soldier's. You were a true man of principles A.J. Baddick and God Bless You. I hope some day in Heaven I can shake your hand and thank you so much for all that you are and the legacy you leave us with."

-Tiff4 U.S. Army of Statesboro, Georgia.

KEEPING BUSY

Chapter 16

I was at breakfast one morning with some very good friends of mine, Paul and Ruth Gordon. I met Paul and Ruth a few years ago at the World War II Weekend at the Reading Airport. I was reading an article about the man seated behind the table, who was a prisoner of the Germans during WWII after being shot down in a B-17 bomber. This guy was a belly gunner and had to bail out over occupied France. The article went on to say that Paul was a Berks County resident. I struck up a conversation with the man and told him I also was a Berks County resident but that I was a transplant. He told me he was a transplant too and asked me where I was from originally. I told him, "Tamaqua." Paul said, "you have got to be shittin' me." I said, "why?" He replied, "because that's where I grew up." Holy mackerel, we started asking each other if we knew this guy and that guy, and this place and that place. Well, we have become good friends and have shared quite a few breakfasts together and cookouts at our house. And coincidentally, they live very near to my in-laws, Donald and Gloria Moatz. Donald is also a WWII veteran who served in the Army. He went off to basic training in July, 1945, at Camp Crowder, near Joplin, Missouri. From there he was sent to Fitzsimons Army Medical Center in Denver, Colorado, to be trained as a medic. After completing his training he was transferred to Camp Beale, California. Then it was off to Germany where he served with the 130th Medical Battalion as a hospital technician in the Army Hospital at Heidelberg. During his time there, Donald had the opportunity to visit Berchtesgaden, where Adolf Hitler's mountain residence, the Berghof, was located. He served until the end of 1946.

Well, we were leaving the diner and Ruth pointed to a flyer posted on the wall that described an organization called Berks Enduring Freedom. It said they were accepting donations to send to our troops overseas, and that they had a meeting coming up and were looking for new members. I had been looking for something to get involved in to pass the time and somehow help our military. This seemed to be right up my alley. I went to the next meeting and was welcomed with open arms and a big hug from the founder, Simone Sauers. There is a lot of work involved but it is very rewarding. A shipment was scheduled for Christmas and all the donations and boxes and volunteers went to the Topton American Legion for a week of packing. By the time we finished, approximately one thousand packages were sent to our troops. Some boxes were sent to hospitals, some to soldiers from Berks County, and some to men and units whose names were supplied from various sources. I had a contact name for a Lt. Colonel in the 82nd Airborne in Afghanistan. We sent packages to Lt. Colonel Kurt Ryan and he distributed them for us. Some of his men were in such remote areas in the mountains of Afghanistan, that he arranged for the packages to be air dropped by parachute. He sent us photos of the packages coming down by parachute. I made arrangements for cigars to be sent to Lt. Colonel Ryan from the Thompson and J.R. cigar stores. We later received a photo of Lt. Colonel Ryan and some of his men, standing on a blown up building, weapons slung, berets on their heads, smoking their cigars. It was such an awesome photo that J.R. Cigars used it for the cover on their next magazine. I had the pleasure of meeting Lt. Colonel Ryan on a visit to Ft. Bragg the following year. He is a true military leader and has recently been promoted to full bird Colonel. After completing a course at the Carlisle War College, Colonel Ryan was assigned as Commander of the 10th Mountain Division, Sustainment Brigade at Ft. Drum, New York. Bob Sandri and I were invited to attend the change of command ceremony. While we were there Bob and I were warmly welcomed by Colonel Ryan's wife, Jennifer and their daughter Madison at their home. Kurt and Jennifer are formerly from Pennsylvania, Hanover and Pottsville, respectively.

I have also met another individual who was in Afghanistan when the packages arrived and he was in charge of logistics for the parachute drops. He is Colonel Mike Peterman and he was also at the Carlisle Barracks. Both these men have joined our chapter of the 82nd Airborne Association, the Central Pennsylvania Chapter, Harrisburg. It is an honor and a privilege to know them and have them as members of our association.

After A.J. died I decided to make a CD in his memory. I called it Patriotic Rock and chose songs I deemed appropriate, such as Proud to be an American and The Great Defenders by Lee Greenwood, The Taliban Song and If I Were Jesus by Toby Keith, along with American Soldier and Brought to You Courtesy of the Red, White, and Blue. This Ain't No Rag by Charlie Daniels, and one of A.J.'s favorite songs, Start The Car by Jude Cole.

I asked about getting some copies made and one of the people in the group had connections to get about two hundred made. I typed a small explanation to place in each one and they were put in the packages. Here are a few of the replies:

"To Andrew's father, your package and CD meant so much to my son, in Afghanistan today....we thank you and pray for your son and send love."
-The Alvey Family of Alexandria, Virginia

"Andrew, though I never knew you, I was on active duty in Iraq in 2003 when you gave your life. It is now June of 2008, and I am in Afghanistan continuing to serve our country as a contractor. Today I received a 'To Any Soldier Package,' and guess what was in it? A note and a music CD from your father, Joe Baddick. He somehow has the strength to continue to support the troops, despite losing you. He writes that song number twelve was your favorite, and I am listening to it right now. He didn't write his address in the letter, but I will search for it and write him a thank you letter. Just

wanted you to know, You will always be loved and remembered by your family, your friends, and your country."
-J.L. Alvey of Bahgram, Afghanistan

"Dear Andrew, today I received a package from back home and inside was a CD your father made. After reading the note that accompanied it, I immediately started to listen to it and I began to cry. What a nice CD, and it says that #12, Start the Car by Jude Cole was your favorite. I love that song and will listen to it many times. Thank you for your sacrifice A.J. God Bless You and your family."
-Karen W. in Rhamadi, Iraq

I even shipped a few packages on my own. My best friend, Mike Barnes, a guy I first met when I started my career with the Dept. of Corrections back in 1986, is a member of the Pa. National Guard's 131st Transportation Company. He was deployed twice and I shipped him so much stuff I got an award from his unit, The Army National Guard Team Medal.

Another organization I have become involved with is T.A.P.S. (Tragedy Assistance Program for Survivors.) One day I was reading a recent issue of TAPS and there was a story inside about their Peer Mentor program. It sounded interesting and as I read on it explained how family members that had lost a loved one could volunteer to assist those that were now going through the grieving process. I asked Sheila what she thought and she immediately said that I would be good at doing something like that. I thought about it for awhile and one day I asked my daughter, Elizabeth, what she thought. "Oh dad," she said, "you'd be great at that, do it." There was an upcoming seminar scheduled for the Memorial Day weekend in Washington, and we were already going to be there so I decided to attend their Peer Mentor training class. I met some of the most remarkable people, all of them going through the same sad circumstances. By the end of the day I had heard many different stories of how their loved ones had died but learned we all shared a common bond.

I met two wonderful women who run the seminars, Bonnie Carroll and Darcie Sims. Bonnie became the founder of TAPS following the death of her husband, Brigadier General Tom Carroll, in a C-12 plane crash in 1992. Darcie Sims, Ph.D., CHT, CT, GMS, is an internationally recognized speaker on the subjects of grief and bereavement, and is a bereaved parent herself. She is the author of "Why Are The Casseroles Always Tuna?", "Footsteps Through The Valley", "Touchstones", and "If I Could Just See Hope." She was also coping editor for Bereavement Magazine for 15 years. She is now the editor for Grief Digest. Darcie is president and co-founder of Grief Inc., a grief consulting business, and the Director of the American Grief Academy in Seattle, Washington. She is the Director of Training and Certification for TAPS. She is listed in Who's Who in America, The World Who's Who of Women and The International Who's Who of Professional and Business Women.

These women and the other terrific staff at TAPS sent me on a journey that I never expected. I have been asked to get in touch with fathers, like myself, that lost their sons, and at times, it is very hard. At other times it can be quite rewarding. I listen to their stories, and they listen to mine. I let them know that as time goes on, they will never forget their loved ones, but it will get better, for I am living proof of that.

I was asked to get in touch with a gentleman from the Baltimore area, Frank Curreri, whose son had recently died. I mulled it over in my head and was thinking that I couldn't do this anymore, it was getting to me. I spoke to Sheila about it and she told me I should do what I thought was best. I was out back, sitting on the deck and thinking about it, when all of a sudden I picked up the phone and called Frank. Thank God I did, because it turned out to be just the phone call to change my mind. I introduced myself and told Frank the reason for my call. I asked him to tell me about his son, Joseph. He started to tell me that Joseph was in the Special Forces, and they had been doing some training at a lake in the Philippines. After the training ended and they were back at their barracks, Joseph realized he had lost the Saint Christopher Medal his grandmother, Ida Curreri, had given him. He grabbed his swim fins and mask and headed back to the lake in search of the medal. Hours later, Joseph's body was discovered. Somehow he had drowned.

I then told Frank my son's middle name was Joseph, and that he too, had drowned, over in Iraq. The curious thing was that my mother had given me a Saint Christopher Medal when I entered the military and I passed the medal on to my son, Andrew, when he joined the Army. So basically, it was from his grandmother, Rose.

When I called Frank I never imagined that our son's stories would be so intertwined. I'm so glad we had a chance to talk on the phone and I look forward to meeting Frank and his wife, Trish. Frank has cordially invited us to come to their house, where Frank says he will treat us to some of his fine cooking. Being a peer mentor has been good for me, and I am glad I chose to become part of the TAPS family. There is a motto at TAPS that reads, "Remember the Love, Celebrate the Life, Share the Journey." For me, that says it all, for I do remember the love I have for my son each and every day, I celebrate the life that still goes on, especially with my family and my grandchildren, and I certainly share the journey by being a member of TAPS, attending seminars with other families, and reaching out to other bereaved fathers.

On a recent trip to Philadelphia to attend a TAPS seminar I had the privilege to speak to some brand new Gold Star families. Some spoke of the guilt they had for not trying to stop their loved one from going to war (one mother actually said she had a plan to kidnap her son to prevent him from deploying), or the anger they had toward the president, government, or military.

I took a moment to speak, and I told them that perhaps I was an exception to the rule, for I never had anger or guilt. I knew that my son died doing exactly what he loved, being a member of our military, serving with pride, and knowing that his Commander in Chief could send him anywhere in the world, and if that meant going into harm's way, then so be it. I finished my statement with, "if what I just said helps any of you deal with the guilt and anger, I will be glad." A.J.'s niece, Andi Rose, accompanied us and is becoming quite the celebrity in the TAPS community. More than a few of the staff remembered her from last year and went out of their way to make her visit memorable.

The seminar was funded by the Travis Manion Foundation and hosted by Tom and Janet Manion, parents of Lt. Travis Manion, USMC, killed by a sniper in the Al Anbar Province of Iraq, April 29, 2007. When asked why he had to deploy for a second time, Travis simply said, "If not me, then who?"

It has become the motto of the foundation. Since many Gold Star families traveled some distance to attend, some as far away as California, the Manions decided to give all of us a "taste of Philly." Dinner included Philly cheese steaks and pizza. All of us were given Phillies shirts and Eagles key rings. The highlight of the evening was a surprise concert by the local Mummers Band. A grand time was had by all in attendance.

KENTUCKY BLUEGRASS

Chapter 17

On July 13, 2009, Sheila and I had the opportunity to meet with the family of Sgt. Darrin Potter for the very first time. There are many positive reasons for the writing of this book. However, meeting the family of the soldier who shared my son's fate was, for me, a meeting that was long overdue, and simply a wonderful experience.

We arrived at the Potter residence in Louisville, Kentucky, and received a warm welcome from Darrin's father, Dave, and his mother, Lynn. We were ushered into a beautiful home and I immediately noticed, over in the dining room, a tribute to Darrin. This was not too dissimilar from what we have in our own home in honor of A.J. There was a folded American Flag in a display case, along with a set of Sergeant stripes, medals, unit patches, and photos.

Lynn presented us with a wonderful assortment of gifts; there was a miniature Louisville Slugger baseball bat, a small bag of Kentucky bluegrass seeds, a bottle of Maker's Mark Bourbon flavored BBQ sauce, a bottle of

Kentucky Straight Honey (100% pure), some delicious chocolates, and a genuine dirty ol' horseshoe from Churchill Downs. We loved it.

We sat down and began speaking of our sons. We learned that Darrin had been a member of the Kentucky National Guard's 223rd Military Police Company for five years. He was the first Kentucky National Guardsman to die in a combat situation since the Vietnam War, and was twenty four years old. Dave told us that he had just spoken to Darrin on the morning of his death. I asked them if they remembered their initial reaction to the news, because I remembered thinking and hoping that the military machine had made some mistake in identifying which soldiers had died that night. You keep hoping that another call will come with an apology that a mistake had been made. But that would not be the case. Dave had been at work and received a call that there was a family emergency and could he get right home? He said he knew at that point that Darrin had either been injured or had died. When he arrived home there were two officers in full dress and they expressed to him that his son had been killed in action. They said they had another set of officers en route to Lynn's workplace to inform her. Dave said he then called her and at that point she didn't know, but Lynn said she detected something in Dave's voice, and she knew he was upset. She asked him if he was congested and he said no, that he was on his way to her office. Lynn told him, "No, just go ahead and tell me, what's wrong?" Just then, a co-worker came in and told Lynn there were Army officers downstairs to see her and then she knew. She knew the awful news about her son without even being told.

We were also joined by Anita, Darrin's younger sister, and Keith Harned. Dave said no two kids could have been closer. Darrin wore a picture of his sister around his neck. Lynn told us that there were two things you could never, ever talk bad about around Darrin, that was his sister and his car. She also said that as young children, she would make them sit together on the steps and hug when they weren't seeing eye to eye. Anita told us that when mom wasn't looking, there would be a lot of pinching and hair pulling.

Keith was also a member of the 223rd M.P. Company and served with Darrin in Iraq. Keith was actually on the mission that night and was in the lead vehicle. At some point, his vehicle stopped, because they realized the other vehicles weren't following them. By the time they turned around and returned to where the humvee went into the water, Darrin and A.J. were already swept under the bridge. Keith reported to us, that, in conversation with the others in the humvee, he was told that Darrin kept a cool head, saying, "hold on guys, just let the vehicle fill with water and it will be easier to exit it." These were up-armored humvees, very heavy, and impossible to get the doors open with the water around them. They had no choice but to make their exit through the turret, as Darrin had directed.

Keith said Darrin loved what he was doing. He believed in his mission and he loved to travel, anywhere. They saw the site where the tower of Babel once stood, and the Tigris and Euphrates rivers. They also visited the ruins of Ur, situated near the town of Nasiriya, south of Baghdad. Ur means "city" in Sumerian, and was the capitol of the ancient civilization. It is also believed to be the birthplace of the prophet Abraham. This part of the world is where civilization began, and for Darrin, having a religious background, it was a huge opportunity to see the things he did. In his short life, Darrin visited eighteen countries thanks to the National Guard. A deployment to Bosnia allowed him to see most of Europe. At this point we all decided that there were many similarities between our sons, and that they looked at the military as a way to see the world in a way many of us never would.

Keith said that Darrin made a lot of connections. He was the kind of guy that people naturally took to. Darrin and A.J. certainly had similar personalities.

Keith told us a story about how, the whole time they were over in Iraq, Darrin would always have Kool-Aid with him, and when Keith would ask him for some, Darrin would reply, "sorry man, this is my last one." Keith said this would happen all the time. When Darrin died, Keith had to help go though his personal items and low and behold, there was a huge stash of Kool-Aid.

Keith told us they had some really wild times in Iraq. On one mission transporting prisoners, one of them died from dehydration, and a remark was made that, "oh well, guess he didn't drink enough." On another occasion, Keith said they were sent on a mission to get a humvee worked on. Darrin told Keith that there was a Kid Rock concert nearby and they were going to it. Keith was a bit concerned about that, but Darrin put him at ease saying he would accept full responsibility. When they returned to base, Darrin did take full responsibility, and Keith said Darrin lost a bit of his ass, but that was Darrin's way. You didn't hesitate to put your trust in him.

Keith went on to tell us about the Abu Ghraib prison scandal. He said that no one ordered those soldiers to do what they did. They were just soldiers goofing off and having a good time. The photos of the prisoner standing on a box, with a hood over his head and wires attached to his fingers was a hoax. There wasn't even electricity in the prison, it was a very old and basic facility. I told the Potters that when I saw that particular photo, my thoughts were that the hooded prisoner could have been one of the insurgents that was firing mortar rounds into the prison, that led to our son's having to go out on a mission that night to stop them. I felt no sympathy for that prisoner and I feel the soldiers who orchestrated the photos got the bum's rush. Those photos showed actions, that in a fraternity initiation, would be considered child's play. Sometimes our leaders just lose sight of who we're fighting out there. These people want to kill us, not just kill us, but, annihilate us. God help us all.

I've always been a believer that the Lord works in mysterious ways. Through Darrin's death, Keith and Anita have become husband and wife. When asked what her brother might have thought about her marriage to Keith, she stated, "I'm sure Darrin would want me to be happy and he would have approved." Keith just said, "He'd kill me." They are a lovely couple and we wish them all the best.

I asked the Potter's what their feelings were about Iraq, now that their son had died. Lynn said that she felt she had to believe that Darrin had made a difference over there, and that perhaps it wouldn't be known for a few years, but that down the road the Iraqi people would be totally free and have good lives thanks to Darrin's efforts. She said that other National Guardsmen returning home have told her that they are making a difference in the lives of the Iraqi people. Dave said that he didn't think the Iraqi people would ever know democracy the way we know it, but on the other hand, no people should live in bondage. Keith stated that we are not only over there to free the people's bodies, but to also free their minds. To give them the opportunity for an education, free from oppression.

Lynn told us there was a letter circulating around the time of Darrin's death that he not only gave his life for the Iraqi people, but also to keep us safe, here at home, because there has never been a successful terrorist attack on our shores since 9/11.

Sgt. Darrin Potter is buried in Cave Hill Cemetery, Louisville, Kentucky. The cemetery has some prominent figures including Colonel Harland Sanders of Kentucky Fried Chicken fame. Also, John Bull, known for his worldwide patent of a sarsaparilla remedy following the Civil War. When his medicine failed him, Dr. Bull gave up smoking, and immediately died.

I closed our meeting by saying that although it was an awful way for us to meet, I felt that Darrin and A.J. were together, and smiling, because our two families had finally met. I believe that, had Darrin and A.J. met, they would have become the best of friends.

SIBLINGS

Chapter 18

I asked my daughter, Elizabeth, if there were some memories of her brother that she'd like to add to his book. The following is what she wanted to share with those of you reading this:

> "I remember waking up the morning after I found out A.J. died, not sure if his death was a dream or reality. Then I realized it was real, it was the worst moment of my life.
>
> I remember making a comment to a newspaper reporter after his death saying, 'he feared nothing, there was no hesitation in him', I truly believe this.
>
> One thing I will always remember from his viewing, in addition to the thousands of people that came to pay their respects, was that there were people from all walks of life, from doctors and lawyers, to people who hadn't gotten off their bar

stools in years. His death touched so many people. I think that speaks volumes as to his character.

When we were making his funeral arrangements, the funeral director called to tell us that Heisler's had contacted him and offered their horse and buggy for the funeral procession. We thought he would have liked that so we said 'yes.' After A.J. was buried, my parents each received a 'final letter' from him. My mom's letter mentioned calling Heisler's regarding the horse and buggy, something he never told anyone before.

A.J. always wanted to be buried at Arlington if something should happen to him. I never understood why, it seemed so far from home. I know why now. Arlington is a place of honor and prestige. I am reminded of that each time I visit.

After A.J. died, one of my friends told me that our children will read about him and others like him someday, she was right.

I found out recently that one of my friends got a tattoo with his name. It makes me feel good to know that people haven't forgotten my brother and they miss him too.

I loved my brother and I know he knew that. The only regret I have is that I'm not sure he knew just how proud I was of him.

A.J. and I grew up as bitter enemies, as many siblings do. The sky was the limit as to the names we would call each other. God help the person, though, that said something bad about my brother or his sister. Of course, we never showed each other how much we cared, but I remember the specific day we became friends. We were both at a party when he was 19 or 20. I was late getting there, but when I finally did get there people kept telling me how worried he was about me. When he saw me he hugged me like he never did before. We hung out together all night. It was one of the most memorable nights of my life.

He was lost for many years and could not find that thing he excelled at. School wasn't his thing, neither was wrestling, football, or many of the other things he tried. Then he found the Army, the thing he was born to do. The Army truly changed him from a boy into a man.

A.J. got married while he was in the Army, and we decided to have a wedding shower and reception for them. The night of the shower, his new wife decided she was not going to participate. I was really angry because we had spent a lot of time planning and preparing for the celebration. Myself and two of my closest friends (people A.J. had known forever), pulled him outside and told him, the next time he got married, he should find someone older than 13 (the age his wife was acting). His response was simply 'O.K.' I realized then that even though we were both adults, what I said still mattered to him. Even though things did not go as planned that night, it was still one of my favorite nights. We ended up with a small group of our old friends standing around telling 'A.J. stories' all night. The drinks were flowing and so were the stories. Stories like the time A.J. stole beer out of my mom's refrigerator and sold it to some of his friends. He watched where they hid it, and when they left, he stole it back and put it back in the refrigerator.

They had a brief marriage and he took the divorce pretty hard. The morning after we buried A.J., we noticed on the morning news that a beer truck had overturned in Cranberry Township in Pittsburg, the town his ex-wife came from.

Even though my daughter never met my brother (maybe she did, in heaven, before arriving here on earth), I can see him in her. Certain ways she turns her head, different facial expressions she makes, even the way she lays on the couch. Coincidence, maybe, but it comforts me to think that maybe part of him is still here with us.

Although I miss him every day and I miss the fact that I don't have my only sibling here to share my life with as I grow old, I don't think he would have wanted things to happen any other way. He is a true hero to his family, friends, town and country. Few people have the opportunity to die doing what they love. My brother was lucky enough to do that."

As I drew near to completing this book, my daughter, Elizabeth, gave birth to her second child, a boy named T.J., Tyler Joseph. He was born November 5, 2009 and weighed in at 8 lbs. 2 oz. When I first held him in my arms, I thought about the years to come, and how Tyler would learn all about his uncle A.J. from us, and from this book. I'm wondering if Andi Rose and T.J. will get along or will there be friction between them like the kind their mother and uncle A.J. experienced. Only time will tell, but it sure will be interesting to see in years to come. Coincidentally, Elizabeth and A.J. were five years apart and now Andi Rose and T.J. are five years apart. Also, Elizabeth was the older sibling, and now Andi Rose is the older sibling. God has been good to us.

HEROES

Chapter 19

You read and hear a lot about heroes in a lifetime, but do we fully realize what a hero is? There's Batman, Superman, Spiderman, Wonder Woman, and the rest who are dubbed superheroes. But they aren't real, so are they really heroes? I suppose they are in the realm of the fantasy world. They go around rescuing people, capturing the villains, and saving the world from destruction. But in the real world, what is a hero? Heroes come from all walks of life and most never intend to become one. I believe the men and women who are engaged in the war on terror in Iraq and Afghanistan are heroes, one and all. They are living heroes, much like those who put their lives in jeopardy every day, fighting fires and responding to 911 police calls. We walk among heroes on the street and never even know it. However, they are the living heroes.

What about those that have passed on? Heroes like Major John Pryor, a University of Pennsylvania trauma surgeon, who dashed to the heart of Ground Zero on September 11, 2001, to volunteer his services. On his second tour of duty in Iraq, with the 344th Combat Support Hospital, Major Pryor was returning to his living quarters after attending mass on Christmas Day, 2008, when an insurgent rocket took his life. He was quoted as saying, "In Iraq, ironically, I found myself drawing on my experience as a civilian trauma surgeon each time mass casualties would overrun the combat hospital. As nine or ten patients from a firefight rolled in, I sometimes caught myself saying, just like another night in West Philadelphia." A quote from Albert Schweitzer hung on Dr. Pryor's Penn office wall that reads:

> "Seek always to do some good, somewhere. Even if it's a little thing, do something for those who need help, something for which you get no pay but the privilege of doing it. For remember, you don't live in a world all your own. Your brothers are here, too."

It would seem that Major John Pryor lived and died by those words.

How about Chief Petty Officer Lance Vaccaro, a Navy Seal, who risked his life numerous times on several missions into Iraq and Afghanistan? Although he was veteran of 300 parachute jumps, he would lose his life in a parachute training exercise in Arizona.

How about Specialist Kristofor Stonesifer. As a member of the 75th Ranger Regiment, Kristofor died in a Blackhawk helicopter crash in Pakistan. They were assigned a supporting role for U.S. Special Forces in Afghanistan. Kristofor was awarded the Bronze Star and

Purple Heart. His Mother Ruth, who heads the Pennsylvania Gold Star Mothers, was instrumental in getting legislation passed allowing Gold Star Families to have their own special license plate.

What of Sgt. Matt Sandri or Sgt. Darrin Potter? How about Specialist T.J. Barbieri or PFC Robert Dembowski? Heroes all, and I would bet not one of them ever aspired to be a hero. But nonetheless, they are and they will always be remembered in that way - as heroes. Heroes will always be around, but for me, my number one hero of all time is my son, Sgt. Andrew J. Baddick. Thank you for 'the little while.' I love you son. God bless you.

EPILOGUE

Meeting Sharon Wells Wagner has taken me on a very special journey in my life. She believes there are no coincidences, that everything happens with a purpose. She has made me a true believer and I know, now, that this book had to be written; otherwise we would never have met.

Losing my father in 2002, my son in 2003, and my mother in 2004 hit me like a shock wave. Three of the people I loved most, gone, in what I considered just a moment in time.

People have asked me how I handled the death of my son and my response has always been, "I never could have done it without my wife Sheila, my family, my dear friends, and my belief in God. They were my support group, they kept me sane, they gave me the help I needed to carry on. But I didn't just want to carry on, I wanted to do something productive, something that would help others, through A.J.

Joining Berks Enduring Freedom was the first step, and then came TAPS. I realized that I had the ability to reach out to others who were just going through the pain I had endured, and let them know that there is hope, that life goes on, and the pain would lessen. I look forward to meeting new Gold Star Families when we attend seminars and visit A.J.'s gravesite in Arlington. I shake more hands when I notice a veteran. I have attended funerals of local soldiers who have died, and introduced myself to their grieving families. All of these things have been a panacea for me. Those who have not lost a loved one unexpectedly, can never know our pain, we Gold Star Families. How we deal with the pain is different for all of us. My way of alleviating the pain has been by reaching out to others.

Writing this book has been a journey for me, back to happier times, interesting times, fun times, and sad times. In talking to other families, I found out that our sons led very similar lives. They were loving, humorous, dedicated, professional, and seemed to be cut from the same special cloth that made them who they were, a breed apart from all others.

My hope is that this book will be therapeutic for some, and for others, just good old, couldn't-put-it-down reading.

PHOTOGRAPHS

A.J. and big sister Liz.

A.J. around 2 years old.

The author's mother playing Mister Interlocutor in a
minstrel show.

Joe, Jesse, Frank

Pleasant Row during the Indian Celebration in Tamaqua.

George Dunstan (L) and Joe Baddick, Sr. (R) during the
Indian Celebration.

Indian Celebration group photo. Standing (from left): George Dunstan, Rose Baddick, Lottie Dunstan, Rose Lewis, Harry Lewis, Joe Baddick, Sr., Tony Lore, Buddy Bell, Mary Lore, and Dolly Lore. Sitting (from left): Dave Dunstan, Jessie Dunstan, and Joe Baddick, Jr.

The author's dad with his shirt pocket full.

Joe Baddick, Sr.'s brothers and sisters. Standing (from L): Helen, Kay, Jean, Eleanor, Eddie. Seated (from L): Frank, Genevieve, Josephine.

Erik, T.J., the author, and A.J.

A.J. around 10 years old.

A.J. the wrestler.

A.J. and Roy "Bud" Krell, Jr.

Elizabeth and Casey.

The author and Donny Krell celebrating Christmas, 1986.

Donny Krell, June, and their granddaughter Emma.

"You'll shoot your eye out, kid!" A.J. at Christmas.

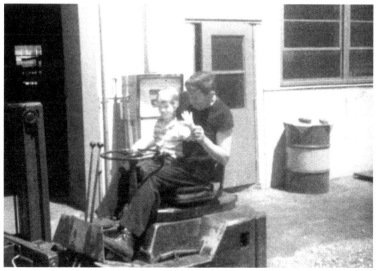

A.J. and Pap, 1980.

The author with A.J. and Liz sporting a black eye from basketball.

A.J. the angler.

The author, Sally Starr, and A.J.

A.J. enjoying his cousin's wedding.

The author and Sheila cutting a rug.

Elizabeth's graduation ceremony at East Stroudsburg University, PA.

Grammy Rose and Christine.

A.J. the hunter.

A.J. in his kayak on the Lehigh River near Jim Thorpe, PA.

A.J.'s Airborne wings tattoo.

Guy and Joe, Sr. with hot wings.

The author's parents, Joe and Rose.

Neighborhood flag raising for A.J.'s deployment.

Christmas with PFC Baddick and Liz.

A.J. with a sniper rifle.

A.J. at Ft. Bragg after a jump.

The author and A.J. at Ft. Bragg after a jump.

A.J.'s favorite picture of himself.

A.J. and Harry.

Kaitlyn sporting an 82nd Airborne hat.

Wedding photo with Gram, Liz, and Shack.

Tyna, Kyle, Rick, and Kaitlyn Dierolf.

Harry.

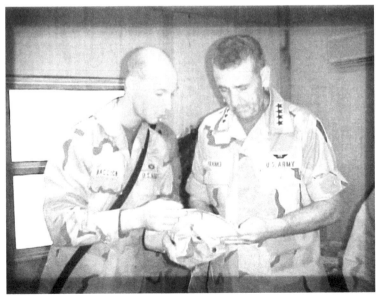

A.J. with General Tommy Franks in Afghanistan.

A.J. and his father's last photo together.

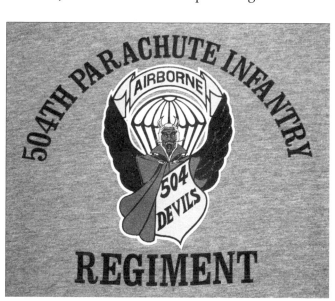

504 Devils – the author's unit and A.J.'s.

A.J.'s Class A uniform with Headquarters Company.

The author in uniform, 82nd Airborne, 1971.

A.J. clowning around in Iraq.

Johnathan Elliott in Iraq.

A.J. in a Humvee in Iraq.

T.J. Barbieri.

Sgt. Darrin Potter at the ruins of Ur.

Zack Kraphl (L) and Alan Meador (R).

Matt Sandri of Shamokin, PA.

Command Sgt. Major Frank Hacker.

Sgt. Michael Wright.

At Arlington with troopers from Headquarters Company.

The incident site near Abu Ghraib Prison, Iraq.

A.J. at Ft. Hood, TX.

A.J.'s memorial service in Iraq.

A.J.'s headstone at Arlington.

The President of the United States of America, authorized by an Act of Congress, July 2, 1926, has awarded the Soldier's Medal to

SERGEANT ANDREW J. BADDICK
UNITED STATES ARMY

FOR HEROISM:

above and beyond the call of duty on 29 September 2003, while saving a fellow Soldier from drowning near Abu Gharayb, Iraq. Without hesitation or regard to personal safety, Sergeant Baddick entered the treacherous waters to rescue a drowning soldier. After securing that Soldier, Sergeant Baddick proceeded to rescue another drowning Soldier, but was unable to overcome the force of the current. He was swept away, giving the ultimate sacrifice in an effort to rescue another Soldier. Sergeant Baddick's extraordinary heroism in the face of imminent danger reflects great credit upon himself, the Red Devils, Task Force Panther, the 82d Airborne Division, and the United States Army.

A.J.'s Soldiers' Medal certificate.

A.J.'s medals: Bronze Star and Soldier's Medal.

A.J.'s awards.

A Co. 1st Battalion 504th Memorial at Ft. Bragg.

The Global War On Terrorism Memorial at Ft. Bragg.

A.J.'s memorial at Patrick Sowers' store in Dallas, TX.

A.J.'s portrait done by Michael Reagan.

The author and Sheila with President Bush at Ft. Bragg.

President Bush holding Andi Rose.

Bob Sandri (L), the author, and Col Kurt Ryan (R).

T.J. Barbieri's dad.

Sheila with Annette Sandri and her daughter Lydia.

The author, General Jefforey Smith, and Bob Sandri.

The author and Mike Barnes at World Tour, Myrtle Beach.

Veterans' Day 2007, Washington, DC.

The author and Sheila with Sgt. Darrin Potter's parents.

Rich Campbell, Ricky Campbell, Nephew Greg, the author, and Guy.

At a TAPS seminar with Bonnie Carroll and Darcie Sims.

A.J.'s godmother Joann Palawsky, her sister Jean, and their mother Eleanor.

The author and Sheila with Paul and Ruth Gordon.

Donald and Gloria Moatz.

The author's Uncle Eddie (L), New Guinea, WWII, 11th Airborne.

Andi Rose and her Pappy dancing.

Kaitlyn with Chief Three Feathers in Washington, DC.

Eagles fans: Liz, Shack, Andi Rose, and T.J.

One happy Pappy with Kaitlyn, Kyle, and Andi Rose.

PHOTO CREDITS

The photographs in this book are courtesy of the author and the following:

Monsignor Thomas Baddick, June and Donny Krell, Elizabeth Hoherchak, Tyna Dierolf, Johnathan Elliott, Tom Barbieri, Dave & Lynn Potter, Bob & Annette Sandri, CSM Frank Hacker, General Jefforey Smith, and Patrick Sowers.

BIBLIOGRAPHY

Operational Fatality Brief by Colonel Jefforey A.Smith, Commanding Officer of the 505th Parachute Infantry Regiment. 2003.

"If You Saw The Pile of Roses" by Francie Dembowski, May 24, 2008. TAPS Magazine, Summer 2008.

Fallen Heroes of Operation Iraqi Freedom @ fallenheroesmemorial.com.

The Catholic Standard and Times. "Ordinary Men, Extraordinary Lives" by Gloria Pinsker. October 2, 2003.

Personal papers and documents.

CONTACT INFORMATION

If you would like to contact the author, please feel free to do so by sending an email to the following address:

JosephBaddick@gmail.com